Chris O'Connell

Junior Sophister

Legal Science

Trinity College

The Nature of Law

---

for Irvine and Diana Smith

The Nature of Law

ALAN WATSON

Edinburgh : at the
University
Press

Edinburgh University Press
22 George Square, Edinburgh

ISBN 0 85224 318 9

Set in Monotype Plantin by
Speedspools, Edinburgh and
printed in Great Britain by
The Scolar Press Ltd
Ilkley, Yorks

Contents

Preface

The argument of this book is that the distinguishing and sole necessary feature of law is the availability of an institutionalised process, which has the essential function of resolving actual or potential disputes, by means of a decision, with the specific object of inhibiting further unregulated conflict. An essential function is defined as one whose failure cannot be structured into the system or whose constant failure cannot be accepted as tolerable. The essential functions of legal rules are to enable the process to be called into being and to validate—not necessarily determine—the decision. The essential functions of law, therefore, to relate to order.

No other features or functions—including the maintenance of justice and liberty—are necessary to law except in so far as their absence would cause a failure of the essential functions. Justice and freedom are preserved by law neither more nor less than the particular society requires and permits.

In conformity with this approach it is maintained that primitive law, International law, and the rules of a trade union or other group, can rightly be regarded as law. But law contains a wealth of features that are not revealed in the essentials, and Western jurists would single out particular attributes as typical of law. These typical attributes are to be found above all in the law of a national state and this from a Western viewpoint should therefore be seen as law *par excellence*. Attributes that further any of the essential functions are particular virtues of law.

Many legal rules channel human behaviour. But if the sole essentials of law relate to order then it follows that even these legal rules will by no means inevitably reflect the political, social and economic needs and desires of the members of the society as a whole or of its ruling élite. A close correspondence between legal rules and the needs and desires of members of a society or its rulers is indeed lacking in practice.

To fulfil its essential rôle relating to order, law needs to have some authority and this is supplied by force (or violence) and respect. Law does not cease to be law because it requires to be backed by force. Indeed, the law of a nation state that is not backed by force is unthinkable. But it is possible for some 'lesser' forms of law to exist without the backing of force and be maintained solely by respect for the law.

Part of the argument in the final three chapters has developed from previous work of mine. Chapter 6, indeed, is largely an abridged restatement of *Society and Legal Change* (1977). Chapter 7 looks again at the phenomenon of legal borrowing, although from a different standpoint from that in my *Legal Transplants* (1974). And respect for law, which is touched on in that book, is the subject of chapter 8.

I owe much to many friends especially to those who read the whole typescript and gave me the advantage of their criticisms; Mr John Barton, Mr Robert Black, Mr Jonathan Cohen, Professor A. M. Honoré, Mr Sandy McCall Smith, Professor Neil MacCormick, Professor Gian Poggi and Mr Archie Turnbull. The last, Secretary of the Edinburgh University Press, has kept a sharply benevolent eye on the whole venture, of which the initial idea was his own.

As often before, Mrs Mary Schofield coped admirably with my untidy manuscript.

ALAN WATSON
Edinburgh
March
1977

I

The Essential Function of Legal Process

(I)

'Tell me, what is law?', asked Socrates,[1] and the question continues to be put. There are many theories of law and its nature; definitions of law—themselves based expressly or impliedly on a theory—are at least as numerous. The major theories, in their turn, are subdivided into varieties, each of which has its own proponents who reject the other varieties. It will not be my purpose here to offer a critique of any of the existing approaches to understanding the nature of law. Yet the three main approaches, namely Natural Law, Legal Positivism, and Law as Social Control, all contribute to the argument of this book; and, to the extent that they do, I should like at this stage to say a word—no more—about them. All of them, naturally enough, contain valuable insights for any understanding of law. The basic tenet of Natural Law is that whether a rule is or is not law depends on its nature as a commandment of god or on its moral quality, not on its creation or acceptance by a particular human society. The idea of Natural Law has a long and distinguished history. It appears in virtually its classic form as early as the Platonic or pseudo-Platonic dialogue *Minos*:[1] law is noble, and seeking after it is a good; but of a city's resolutions some are good, some are evil; law is not evil, hence an evil resolution of a city is not law. Already, that is, we have both the classic idea that an evil resolution is not law, and the appeal to an outside standard—in the *Minos* the appeal is not absolutely express but is to justice—to determine what is or is not law. This appeal may be to revealed religion, to right reason, and so on, depending on the individual proponent of the theory. The two main problems for Natural Law also already make their appearance in the *Minos*. How can a resolution that is passed in the same way as law and is enforced in the same way as law, and is treated by the

state as law, reasonably be claimed not to be law? Why can one not admit it is law but bad law? Secondly, to determine whether a resolution is or is not law how can one appeal to a standard outside the political structure that passed the resolution? And how can one agree on the outside standard to which appeal is to be made? On this latter aspect it should be emphasised that no agreement has been reached, and there seems no way in which agreement can ever be reached. Even if it could be accepted—which in any event it cannot—that one should appeal to divine revelation, and, at that, divine revelation within Christianity, agreement on Natural Law would still not exist. For instance, even within the Roman Catholic tradition the stance of St Augustine on Natural Law[2] is very different from that of St Thomas Aquinas.[3] Again, the views of these theologians on the nature of Natural Law differ greatly from those of the Stoic philosophers,[4] of Thomas Hobbes,[5] of Grotius,[6] and so on.

Yet what must above all be stressed is that Natural Law is emotionally satisfying, vigorous and potent. This is most clearly revealed by the passionate views and moral conduct of persons who are neither lawyers nor philosophers, and who may never have seen or heard a Natural Law doctrine formulated. One might think of some modern instances of civil disobedience; but examples are best drawn from times when—so far as our knowledge goes—no precise theory of Natural Law existed. Thus, even before the *Minos* was written, Sophocles makes Antigone exclaim to Creon's accusation that she was bold enough to break the law:

> Yes, for in my opinion Zeus did not command these laws, nor did Justice who sits with the gods below enact these human laws. Nor did I think that you, a mortal, could annul and override the unwritten and unchangeable laws of the gods. For they are not of today or yesterday . . .[7]

One can cite the still earlier story of the Jewish midwives who hid the male newborn infants contrary to Pharaoh's command that they should be killed: 'But the midwives feared God, and did not do as the king of Egypt commanded them, but saved the men children alive.'[8] Here already is the idea that the laws of men and the commands of God may conflict, and that it is then unwise or wrong to obey the former.[9]

In contrast Legal Positivism insists that a rule is law precisely

because it is created and accepted as such by a particular human society. On this approach the morality or immorality of a rule or any supposition of divine origin is irrelevant to the question whether the rule is or is not a legal rule. For the positivists the historically seminal view is that of John Austin,[10] for whom positive law is the command of a sovereign backed by a sanction. By his definition the command of a sovereign is habitually obeyed. The first drawback to this view and the modern variations of it[11] is the difficulty of fitting International law and primitive law within the concept of law. ('Primitive law' is rather a vague term: it is used here to signify the 'law' of economically underdeveloped pre-literate societies.) It is not always easy to find a person or body who can be regarded as the sovereign, and often in both primitive law and International law there is nothing that can be regarded as a regulated sanction. Yet apart from professional legal philosophers, lawyers happily consider both International law and primitive law as law. Secondly, even in a modern legal system it is not easy to see how custom that becomes law can be treated as a command of a political superior. Yet it can happen, for instance, that a custom practised in a particular locality is accepted by a court as law even in derogation of the common law of the land. But no one ordered the custom: it simply grew up. To fit this into the theory Austin claimed—unconvincingly—that when customs are turned into legal rules by decisions of subject judges the legal rules are *tacit* commands of the sovereign. For my own part I also find something very artificial in emphasising the *command* of a sovereign as the distinguishing mark of a legal rule that exists now but may have come into existence centuries before in very different circumstances. A third and still greater objection, it seems to me, is that the Positivist approach reveals nothing—and is not intended to reveal anything—about the purpose and function of law.[12]

Most prominently associated with the idea of law as a means of social control are the Marxists, who maintain that all law is class law and is made by the economically ruling class with the effect of maintaining its interests. The proponents of the idea have to face the problem that not only are many legal rules socially neutral, but also that, largely as the result of inertia, a very great deal of law is and remains badly out of step with the needs and desires of both society and its ruling élite.[13]

Although theories of Legal Positivism and of Law as Social Control are discussed usually in terms of their modern exposition, both, like Natural Law, have a long and important history. Thus, the idea that law is nothing more nor less than the decision of a political community appears prominently in the *Minos* itself; and it is emphasised in Plato's *Laws*[14] that laws are different in the various states. In that work, too, we find expressed the idea that the legislator might seek to have his instructions obeyed by means of sanctions.[15] In Plato's *Republic*, Thrasymachus insists that the interest of the ruling class determines what is justice in both the moral and the legal sense.[16] Aristotle declares that law may serve the interests of a class,[17] and he considers that the best legislators are from the middle class.[18] Natural Law, Legal Positivism, and Law as Social Control do not need to be analysed further here. But it should be noted that the last view lies on a different conceptual plane from the first two. Natural Law and Legal Positivism argue different answers to one problem: the source of validity of law. Law as Social Control is concerned not with that problem but with the function of law or the source of the content of law.[19]

(II)

There are, as I have said, many approaches to an understanding of the nature of law. If we are to consider something man-made, to decide what it is in its essence, then one reasonable approach is to consider its function in society. Of course, the word 'function' has several meanings, and to use it carelessly and indiscriminately results in confusion.[20] For classical functionalists the 'function' of any recurrent activity denotes 'the part it plays in the social life as a whole and therefore the contribution it makes to the maintenance of the structural continuity'.[21] On this view, all idea of purpose both in the word 'function' and in social institutions is vigorously excluded. The functionalists' theory of social institutions has provoked much opposition—the theory does not easily explain social change, for instance—and is now regarded by many sociologists as discredited.[22] But an approach based on the idea of intended purpose is also not free from theoretical difficulty. If, in discussing what an institution does, one introduces the idea of what it is intended to do one has to grapple with the problem that intention may be manifest or latent, explicit or implicit, conscious or unconscious, impossible or realistic. What people say they intend may not be what they actually do intend, and they may actually intend what is impossible of achievement. If one were to claim that to understand the nature of an institution one must know what it is intended to do, and that therefore one must above all stress realistic intention, one would be involved in a circular argument; in the final analysis, what the institution is intended to do can only be judged by what it actually does.

A third approach to explaining institutions is also at times called a 'teleological explanation'. This is described by Lessnoff: 'In this connection, the idea of teleological explanation is that such laws, which express the tendency of a system to maintain a so-called *goal-state*, explain operations which help to maintain that state. Thus, if one were to ask why human beings shiver and sweat, the teleological explanation would be that they do so *in order to* maintain the normal body temperature of 37°C. The phrase "in order to" does not here imply purpose, only that the organism is so constituted that it does tend to maintain the normal body temperature, by means of various mechanisms including sweating and shivering. Clearly teleological explanation departs markedly from the explanatory patterns discussed so far: the explanandum is explained, not by any antecedent, but by its consequence, the goal-state.'[23] But this explanation, whether applied to biological organisms or social institutions, cannot readily be accepted: above all, as Lessnoff says, it seems odd to offer teleological explanations of phenomena such as sweating and shivering, since they can be explained causally through non-teleological laws.

It is not easy to determine which of these approaches to the nature of a social institution is correct or to decide whether some intermediate view is preferable. Fortunately, in the present context it will not be necessary so to determine or decide. The account of law and the legal process to be given in this first chapter can, I believe, readily be formulated in terms of any of these three approaches. If I may express a personal belief—distinct from any claim of proof or certainty—it is that I favour the second of the above approaches. In my opinion it is impossible to make sense of social institutions except within a framework of human purpose; broadly an Aristotelian view. In this book I will use the word 'function' not only to mean what an institution does, but to express the idea of what an institution is intended to do, and can do.

On an approach to the nature of law through its function, the initial answer to the question 'What is law?' would be 'Law is what law does'.[24] But what does law do? A human institution, as we all know, may well have more than one function, and all its functions are relevant to it. Yet a particular function or functions may, I believe, be absolutely essential to a human institution—unless it performed that function or functions the institution would not exist. For the sake of simplicity let me hereafter call that function the 'essential function'. An attempt to characterise the essential function of law would be worthwhile even if the search prove unavailing. Later on I shall consider the relationship of the essential function to other functions.

To this method of procedure it might be objected that, instead of hunting for an essential function, we should be looking for what Ludwig Wittgenstein called 'family likenesses'. Wittgenstein claimed, for instance, that there is no characteristic that is common to everything called a game, but that this does not mean that 'game' has several independent meanings. 'Game' is a 'family likeness' term. In discussing the activity of 'comparing' he says, 'we find that what connects all the cases of comparing is a vast number of overlapping similarities, and as soon as we see this, we feel no longer compelled to say that there must be some one feature common to them all'.[25] The idea of 'family likeness' is very useful and should not here be passed over without mention, but the idea does not preclude us from searching for essential functions or characteristics in law and the legal process. Nor should we be put off the search by the vague feeling that since Wittgenstein it is 'old-fashioned' to look for any common or essential feature or function. Should any function be found that is common to all forms of law or legal process this would create a presumption that the function in question is of fundamental importance for the notion of law or legal process. The presumption is no doubt rebuttable, but the onus of proof should be on those (if any) who wish to deny real significance to the common function.

It should be made express that on occasion a human institution may fail to achieve its essential function. The term 'function' is here being used, it will be recalled, to denote what something is intended to do, can do, and actually does. The occasional failure to achieve the essential function will not, in my view, make the essential function any less the essential function. But a constant failure to achieve the essential function cannot be accepted by the system as tolerable, nor can the failure be structured into the system. I shall draw an analogy from another field of human achievement. The motor car may have many functions, different ones for different people, and may be used in various ways: it may be a status symbol, an aid to seduction, an object of aesthetic appreciation, a means of transporting people along roads. The last of these I would regard as the essential function of the motor car.[26] It can and does happen that an individual car breaks down and fails to be a particular means of land transport. That would not change the essential function of the car, nor make the car any less a car. But if something was designed in such a way that it would not be that particular means of transport, then it would not be a car because the failure to achieve the essential function of a car was built into it. If, however, a car were designed that would not be a prestige symbol or an object of beauty, and in which seduction would be (virtually) impossible, it would not on these grounds be any the less a car.[27]

To illustrate the significance that I wish to assign to the essential function let me give another example from a different field: the zoologist, wishing to classify animals into, for instance, mammals, birds, reptiles, fish, and so on, will concentrate on the qualities that every member of the particular class has. Thus, an animal will be classified as a mammal only if it is warm-blooded and the female secretes milk with which the new-born of the animal can be fed. Of these two characteristics—essential characteristics let me call them—the first, but not the second, is shared with birds. Most mammals, but not all, are viviparous—the duck-billed platypus lays eggs. Thus, being viviparous is not an essential characteristic of mammals, although it is an extremely important and prominent characteristic of virtually all mammalian species. No zoologist discussing mammals would want to underestimate such important characteristics as their producing live young; but in seeking the prime basic character of mammals he would single out the essential characteristics, and pay especial attention to any that were not shared with other forms of animal life. My endeavour here will not be to identify and list all the functions that law may perform in society, but to isolate the essential function or functions, if any, and see if thereby we can learn anything about the nature of law. The search for the essential function is—in the nature of things—a search for the minimum function. That function will be what law must perform if it is to be law.[28] Moreover, the search will be limited to what the function is, and will not be extended to what it ought to be.

(III)

To find the essential function, to see what law must do in society, we should look above all at law in action, since what law must do is then likely to be most obvious. Law in action is most clearly seen in the legal process and the juristic act, and they alone will be discussed in this chapter.

One cannot start by asking what is the essential function of law in the legal process. Rather, one must ask first what is the essential function of the legal process itself, and only when that is determined can one turn to the other question.

The point of a legal process is the resolution of a dispute, actual or occasionally potential, by means of a decision; to find the essential function we must be more specific. I shall list various possible functions of a legal process, and then by means of examples try to show which functions are not necessarily built into every system of law. If the enquiry is properly conducted, any function not excluded by one or more of the examples will be the essential function. The method is not perfect, and is open to the objection that any list of functions will not be complete. Nevertheless, I shall attempt to include in this central list all functions that might be considered fundamental,[29] and can only hope that someone else will point out any that I have omitted. A further objection to this method is that a wider or deeper search would have revealed examples that would make untenable the idea that any function was essential. This objection, of course, can be levelled at any claim that some particular is an essential element of anything. I can only plead that I have tried hard to find examples that would exclude every listed function from being the essential function of the legal process.

Functions of a legal process are:

1) To resolve the dispute by doing or in order to do justice.
2) To resolve the dispute by establishing the facts and applying the relevant rules of law to them.
3) To resolve the dispute in the interests of the immediately involved parties.
4) To resolve the dispute in the best economic interests of society at large.
5) To resolve the dispute in the best economic, social or political interests of the ruling class.
6) To resolve the dispute with the specific object of inhibiting further unregulated conflict.[30]

In all these the process achieves its function through a decision. It should be observed that not all of the functions listed are necessarily mutually exclusive. Above all function two is different in kind from the other functions. All of the others primarily ask 'With what end in view is the dispute resolved?' Function two may be regarded as being more concerned with means than with ends; and these means might further the ends of any of the other functions.[31] Again, function six is on a different level from the other functions listed. Function six could be combined with any of the others; and especially might it be argued that the essential social function of the legal process is precisely function six combined with any of functions one or three or four or five, and that the list of possible essential functions should therefore be increased. But the possibility of enlarging the list in this way need be considered only if more than one of the listed functions—including numbers two or six—survive the search for the essential function. It should also be noted here that function six is much more precise than simply 'to resolve the dispute'.

When we turn to the examples that may demonstrate that a function is not the essential function, we should remember that what has to be shown by them is not that, for instance, on occasion a judicial process fails to establish the facts and settle a dispute by applying the legal rules to them, but that a whole type of legal process is not designed for or is not properly fit for establishing the facts and settling disputes by applying the legal rules to them.

A) *Trial by battle.* Combat, as a means of deciding a suit, whether criminal or civil, was well established in mediaeval Europe, in England as well as elsewhere. Yet although some people might always claim it as a way both of doing justice and of establishing which of the disputants' case was correct at law, the hollowness of the claim was always known. The system of having a professional champion—even churchmen would have champions on yearly retainers, with additional payments when their services were used—is unthinkable if we suppose a belief that the decision would inevitably go to him whose cause was just. So is the idea of a convicted criminal being granted life and limb by the king in legal form provided he becomes approver to fight and rid the land of a number of malefactors.[32] In the Iceland of *Njal's Saga* Mord Fiddle claims the return of his divorced daughter's dowry from her ex-husband, Hrut, who challenges Mord to single combat for the dowry. Mord consults his friends, and Jorund the Priest advises: 'There is no need for you to ask our opinion; you know well enough that if you fight Hrut you will lose your life as well as the money. Hrut is a successful man; he is great by achievement, and a very great fighter.'[33] Yet the story is not presented as though Mord's legal (or moral) case was the weaker. In a subsequent episode, Hrut, again the defendant but in a different matter, is challenged to single combat by the plaintiff Gunnar, whose case is in difficulty, and this time Hrut receives similar advice to that given to Mord Fiddle.[34]

Thus, if trial by battle is an instance of legal process—and it is[35]—neither of the functions listed one and two can be assumed to be an essential function of the legal process. It is not necessary to examine (for function one) the various meanings of justice, since on any definition the result of this type of process may work injustice.

B) *Modern advocacy in the United Kingdom and the working of legal aid.* In the adversary trial system of the modern United Kingdom, each party to the action has a legal representative, who is reminiscent in many ways of a mediaeval champion. The judge, who takes a far less active rôle than does a continental judge in, say, questioning witnesses, is supposed to know only facts drawn to his judicial attention. Hence, the quality of the counsel on either side may be decisive. But, at least in large part, money decides the quality of the representation available to each side. Legal costs can be very high, and it is not uncommon for one side to be represented by a Queen's Counsel aided by an able junior, while the other has to make do with a relatively inexperienced junior. The unfairness built into the system is in part relieved, in part exacerbated by the possibility of legal aid. Legal aid is not available to the wealthy or, usually, even to the lower middle classes. A professional person will find it financially very difficult to bring or even defend an appeal if his adversary is either wealthy or has been granted legal aid.

Modern advocacy and legal aid in the U.K. demonstrate that functions one, two and three are not essential functions of the legal process.

C) *British jury system*. The jury system in Britain, which finds passionate supporters and opponents, is not satisfactory in all types of cases for establishing the facts and applying the relevant rules of law to them. Thus, before the introduction of the breathalyser test and the creation of a new crime, it was very difficult to persuade a jury to convict on a charge of drunken driving. Likewise, juries do not easily convict in complicated fraud cases, especially where the victim is the Inland Revenue.

The jury system provides additional support for ruling out two as the essential function of the process.

D) *Absence of reconciliation machinery*. In some systems attempts may be made to reconcile the parties in certain types of process, particularly divorce. In other, particularly non-Western, legal systems, there may be a vigorous attempt to reach a decision that both parties find acceptable or, at least, not insulting. The absence of any such reconciliation machinery from most Western actions involves us in holding that it is not essential to a process that it be resolved in the best interests of the immediately involved parties.

Again, the high cost of litigation means that a legal process does not necessarily serve the best economic interests of the parties immediately involved.

Thus, function three cannot be considered the essential function.

E) *Economic costs of modern litigation*. The costs to society at large of maintaining processes can be enormous, and this is nowhere more obvious than in criminal cases, especially in petty crime. Thus, a minor charge of being drunk and disorderly will involve society in the cost of the time of the policeman who made the arrest, and of the judge who hears the case, expenses of the witnesses, running costs of the court room and so on, and yet any fine imposed on the defendant may be minimal (if he can even pay) and the deterrent effect slight. Whatever advantages may accrue to society from the prosecution and conviction of petty criminals the process here cannot be claimed to be in the best economic interests of society at large.

Hence, function four can be excluded from our search.

F) *Actions against a monarch, government, ministers of the government and the executive.* In many, but by no means all, countries actions can be brought by private individuals against the monarch or the government or against governmental ministers or officials. Such actions may be brought as freely as actions against private individuals or they may be restricted in scope, subject matter or in the powers of compelling production of evidence; they may be heard in the ordinary courts of the land or only in special administrative courts. Whatever the restrictions or special nature of the proceedings might be, the very existence of such processes in many lands—especially when they are available against the monarch or government—shows that it is not always built into a process that a dispute is to be resolved in the best social or political interests of the ruling class.

The ingenious argument might, however, be produced that, appearances to the contrary notwithstanding, such actions are in the best social or political interests of the ruling class. It might be claimed that they give the people confidence in the government and provide a safety-valve for emotions that might otherwise erupt into violence. The argument is not wholly convincing. The absence of some of the categories of action provided, for breach of contract or negligent damage, for instance, would have little effect on general public confidence and would not lead to outbreaks of violence. Again, such actions, by the publicity they would attract and by their probing into matters otherwise obscure, might bring to light defects in the monarch or government that in the interests of the ruling body would have been better kept hidden.[36] In so far as the argument is at all persuasive it is that it is in the interest of the ruling class that disputes be settled so that unregulated conflict be inhibited. Thus any positive force in this particular argument would have only the effect of making function five a species of the genus function six.

So we can also exclude function five as the essential function of the legal process.

From the above examples it would seem that the essential function of the legal process is not any of the functions listed as one to five. By the process of exclusion only one function has so far survived the test, that listed as number six, the settlement of a dispute with the specific object of inhibiting further unregulated conflict. This function requires further investigation.

What meaning is to be attributed to the idea that the essential function of the process is 'to inhibit further unregulated conflict'? In the first place the process self-evidently *regulates* the instant dispute and moreover settles it in the sense that the court's decision is authoritative. Rancour may still exist between the parties but the instant dispute is settled. Courts tend to take strong measures against behaviour inimical to their decisions. Secondly, if the instant dispute were not regulated and settled it would naturally continue; it could fester and poison other relationships between the parties, and lead to further unresolved disputes that might erupt in violence. Other persons could be drawn into ever-widening conflicts. Thirdly, the decision serves as an example of what the outcome is likely to be in other similar disputes; hence, persons who may expect to win in these other disputes are more ready to press for a process, while those who are likely to lose are less likely to take their as yet unregulated dispute to extremes. Fourthly, the decision may serve as a warning, especially in criminal cases, that certain kinds of behaviour which give rise to disputes will be punished, hence creating a disincentive. Fifthly, again in criminal cases, the freedom of a losing defendant may be restricted in such a way that he will not be able to engage in conflict-making behaviour in society.

Inevitably, there will be instances where, in resolving a dispute, a process fails to inhibit further unregulated conflict. This will not disturb the thesis unless in some instances the failure can be regarded as built into the system. Are there such instances? The crucial case I would suggest is persecution of a group by law, where one method adopted is to institute processes against the group or its members in order either to incite the state's supporters to violence or to provoke the persecuted group to rebel and be defeated.[37] But it is hard to envisage a situation such as that. To begin with, other simpler and more effective means are available to a government that wishes to provoke internal violence. Secondly, one individual process of that type can be considered only with some difficulty as reflecting a failure built into the system, and a series of such processes cannot readily be visualised. Thirdly, even if there is such a series, this would still represent a very exceptional situation and would in no way correspond to any stable usage. The efficacy of such a series of processes would be very limited. It is difficult to consider that a very exceptional, temporary and inefficient way of dealing with the situation can be regarded as built into the system. Fourthly and most importantly, such processes on any theory or conception of law can be regarded only as abuses. One should not admit that the deliberate abuse of legal process by a government can change the fundamental nature of the legal process. Fifthly, no government wishes to have on its hands permanent internal unrest. Where it provokes violence it does so in order to ensure future stability for its own benefit. It uses present violence to inhibit further unregulated conflict in the future. When such a government seeks to provoke violence through the use it makes of a judicial process, one can still argue that the specific object is to inhibit further unregulated conflict. What I have claimed as the crucial case, and I can think of no others more to the point—although the case of victimless crime may present a problem and will be discussed shortly—can not be thought to represent a failure of function six, which is built into the system. Hence, function six can still be considered the essential function of the legal process.

The same conclusion can be reached by a different and positive route. Legal processes arise from disputes. A dispute that is not settled so as to inhibit future unregulated conflict will give rise to further disputes, which would appropriately be settled by processes that, if they were not settled so as to inhibit future unregulated conflict, would give rise to further disputes, and so on *ad infinitum*. This progression of processes to infinity is avoided only if the specific object of settling a dispute by a process is to inhibit future unregulated conflict.

But what, it must now be asked, is the relationship of the essential function to the other functions of a human institution? The former must be built into the institution, the latter may be but need not be, and may be treated as more or less important. The existence of the essential function does not exclude the existence of any other function. When a function that is not the essential function is treated as very important its failure may cause the failure of the essential function; and in the present context the significance of these other functions is precisely this capacity to act on the essential function. The essential function is society's prime and necessary stake in the institution.

One crucial point that has been established—although there was scarcely a need to do so—is that the finding of facts and the application to them of the legal rules is not the essential function of the legal process. Indeed, as some of the examples make plain, the system does not always hide the fact that the legal rules applied to the facts have at times only very limited significance. Among modern legal theorists, the American Realists—if we may treat disparate personalities as a group[38]—have been very active in claiming and demonstrating 'a distrust of the theory that traditional prescriptive rule-formulations are *the* heavily operative fact in producing court decisions'.[39] (But, significantly, the Realists, with the exception of Jerome N. Frank, accept that to a considerable extent judicial behaviour is predictable.[40])

Yet if it is often clear to the observer that the legal rule is of secondary importance in the legal decision, then it must be, as indeed it is, also clear to the parties. When this is so, the parties seem to accept it. Naturally each party wishes to win his case, but (at least until he loses it) he is not too upset by the secondary position of legal rules. Until he has actually won his case, each party is anxious that the recognised practice—here specifically of the legal process—be kept. What the parties want, that is to say, is above all to win the case, but also the recognised practice of the process to be observed. This recognised practice may, but need not in every system, include the idea that legal rules be apparently given top priority.

It is when attention is focused on the importance of the recognised practice that the views of the Natural Lawyers,

Legal Positivists and those who think of law as a means of Social Control become of immense importance to us. People will feel a deep sense of injury if the recognised practice is not acceptable or is not observed. (Acceptable to whom, whether to the parties, society at large, or a significant section of society, is a question that will be discussed in a moment.) And this sense of injury can prevent the process from fulfilling its essential function.

That the recognised practice be acceptable means to begin with that it must have come into existence by an approved method. For a method to be approved it must rest somehow on authority that is recognised as such and obeyed as such. Whether one likes it or not, this authority has much in common with Austin's idea of a sovereign. Yet the authority need not be the command of a sovereign, but may be, for instance, custom. The authority that is relevant here can also easily be found both in International law and primitive law, and can exist even where a sanction is lacking. Again, for the recognised practice to be acceptable it must not offend too greatly against the ethic—*whose* ethic will appear shortly; and here, in connection with the legal process, there is much in common with the Natural Law theorists. But one problem is avoided. So far as outsiders are concerned, one of the great difficulties facing theories of Natural Law is the appeal to a standard external to the political structure to determine what is law and what is not; and the difficulty is compounded by the absence of any agreement as to what this external standard is, and how appeal should be made to it. For us, concerned with the essential function of the legal process, the relevant external standard will be whatever persuades people that in a particular system the particular process is unacceptable and causes a failure of the essential function, a settlement of the dispute for the benefit of society at large with the specific object of inhibiting further uncontrolled conflict. The uncontrolled conflict need not directly concern the terms of the original dispute. Moreover, for the Natural Lawyers, the words 'too greatly' in the remark that the recognised practice to be acceptable 'must not offend too greatly against the ethic', would be central and provoke discussion and disagreement. On the view proposed here, the words 'too greatly' relate only to matters of fact—what does cause such unrest as actually to give rise to further uncontrolled conflict. Nothing has yet been said to clarify the notion of the people to whom the recognised practice must be acceptable. The matter is best put negatively. The recognised practice must not be unacceptable to a section of the community powerful enough to persuade the community to think again, either because it convinces the community as a whole of the rightness of its disagreement or because the community as a whole is unwilling to stand up for the process in view of this section's disagreement.[41] This latter alternative involves the view of Law as Social Control. But at this level the process operates only negatively as social control. The proceedings and verdict may be disagreeable to society as a whole and to powerful groups and, indeed, be avidly desired by no-one, without the process necessarily becoming unacceptable and failing in its prime function.

It might be objected that this analysis is cynical, that on this approach it does not matter whether or not the judge is committed to the argument and to his decision, and that the process and the legal rule within it amount to nothing more than a 'political' device to keep people quiet. The answer is that a very important function of many, of possibly even the great majority of legal processes is to resolve a dispute by establishing the facts and applying the relevant law. Where this is the case then it is vital that the judge be or appear to be committed to the argument and to his decision, since otherwise, it must be stressed, the essential function of the process would be in jeopardy. Yet it should be emphasised that on occasion it is thought important that a result be obtained different from what could be expected if the relevant legal rules were applied to the facts. Readers of Anthony Trollope will remember the trial of Mr Browborough in chapter 44 of *Phineas Redux*. Browborough was unseated from the Commons after a commission proved there was bribery at his election. But there was no desire that he should be imprisoned. The fact that he bribed voters is made clear to the reader, yet at his trial the judge's 'summing up was very short, and seemed to have been given almost with indolence', the jury 'returned a verdict of acquittal without one moment's delay' and the Attorney-General who had led the prosecution

> was by no means disappointed, and everybody, on his own side in Parliament and on the other, thought that he had done his duty very well. The clean-sweeping Com-

> missioners, who had been animated with wonderful zeal by the nature and novelty of their work, probably felt that they had been betrayed, but it may be doubted whether any one else was disconcerted by the result of the trial, unless it might be some poor innocents here and there about the country who had been induced to believe that bribery and corruption were in truth to be banished from the purlieus of Westminster.

The trial of Mr Browborough is a true example of a process working well. Not only is this discretion observable for a process but it is a characteristic of law that not all its rules will be equally enforced at any time.

For simplicity, I have generally used the singular 'legal process' rather than the plural 'legal processes'. What really is involved is the sum or totality of legal processes or the sum of legal processes of a particular type within a system. If one individual process greatly offended the ideas of morality, or the interests of a powerful group, perhaps little deleterious to the system would result. But each process must be seen as an integral part of the whole. Hence it can happen—but need not happen—that one offensive process may have an effect on the standing of the whole system. The importance of an unreasonable process may be greater than its effects on the parties to the suit.

(IV)

I claimed in passing that the 'point of a legal process is the resolution of a dispute, actual or occasionally potential, by means of a decision'. This demands a little clarification. Usually processes involve actual disputes; but sometimes the disputes are best regarded as merely potential, and processes relating to these fall into two classes. In the first, the law makers—probably as a result of experience—regard particular types of situation as likely to give rise to disputes and so demand the use of a process to declare the legal position of the parties in advance of an actual dispute. In such a case the state itself would typically be one of the disputing parties if a dispute did arise. The classic instances relate to judicial hearings that must be held before trust purposes may be varied or before a curator *bonis* is appointed. Here the belief is that if, without the safeguard of a judicial enquiry, trust purposes, for instance, are varied, prospective beneficiaries are likely to object at some future date, or disputes are likely to arise because the state decides that the variations of purpose made by the trustees indicate some neglect of duty. A case intermediate between actual and potential disputes is to be found in countries that demand that decrees of divorce be granted only after a court hearing even when both spouses wish the divorce and neither would contest the granting of the decree or any other relevant matter. The dispute is potential in that grievances may later arise from matters that were not thought contentious at the time, such as division of property or access to children; and also in that, without accurate recording, the matrimonial status of the parties and the validity of a future marriage might be in doubt. The dispute is actual in so far as it can be regarded as one between the divorcing parties and the state. The state (or a significant part of the population that has legislation on its side) insists for whatever reason that divorce ought not to be granted in the absence of particular circumstances, and that marriages (which necessarily involve the community) cannot simply be ended at the whim of the spouses; and, on this view, the purpose of the divorce action is to resolve the dispute between the couple and the state by demonstrating that the facts required for the divorce are or are not present.[42]

The second class of action involving potential disputes arises where persons find themselves in a situation that is conducive to bad blood, and where the state provides a process that the parties may use if they wish so that future unregulated conflict is inhibited. Roman law supplies two splendid examples. As early as the fifth century B.C. the XII Tables provided an action, the *actio familiae erciscundae*, which could be demanded by any heir for the division of an inheritance among the various heirs. The three arbiters had considerable freedom as to how the assets were to be distributed, and it is worth stressing that the person who brought the action could easily find that he had to give up property he held at the beginning of the action.[43] Again, the action on partnership, the *actio pro socio*, might be brought with the sole purpose of ensuring that the assets be distributed in a regulated fashion among the partners, thus reducing the possibility of conflict.[44]

(V)

When we turn to consider the essential function of law or of rules of law in the context of the legal process, we already know that this essential function is not to determine the verdict since, as we have seen, it is not the essential function of the legal process to establish the facts and resolve the dispute by applying the relevant rules of law to them.

One essential function of law appears at the outset. A claim involving law is absolutely necessary to initiate the legal process. This claim may be of a legal right, or that a legal privilege should be accorded, or that a legal power should be granted. For instance, with respect to the first type of claim, the parties to a dispute may or may not differ as to the relevant facts; and individuals may have long standing grievances against one another, a permanent hatred. But a legal process can be involved only if a party also makes a claim of legal right, although this need not exhaust the complaints between the parties. A claim of legal right is always more than a simple claim of fact; it is a claim that particular facts exist, that they have some correspondence with or dissonance from a standard, rule or principle, and therefore something, which the 'court' has authority to decide, ought to be done or be not done. This claim that something ought to be done or be not done involves a claim of law. The situation is similar where the claim is for a privilege or power. Hereafter, for simplicity, I shall usually mention only the claim of legal right. Thus, a first essential function of law viewed from the process is to get the dispute before the 'court', to turn what may be a private quarrel into something of which society properly takes notice and over which society exercises its authority to inhibit further unregulated conflict. This point is well illustrated when in *Njal's Saga*, after various killings, a proposed settlement against Njal's sons has come to nought:

> Njal and his sons walked back to their booth. 'I have long had the feeling that this case would go badly for us', he said, 'and so it has turned out'. 'Not at all', said Skarp-Hedin. 'They will never have any legal grounds for prosecuting us.' 'Then', said Njal, 'it will end in disaster for everyone.'[45]

Consequent upon this function, once the dispute is before the 'court', the parties and the judges in all types of procedure continue to act as if the central issue was the claim of legal right. In trial by battle, for instance, the battle ostensibly is to determine whose claim is right in fact and in law. Yet we know, and so did many in the Middle Ages, that the outcome of the battle could be determined by other factors. Forensic expertise may determine the decision in a modern law suit and the greater skill may be bought by the wealthier party, but the expertise is ostensibly dedicated to establishing or confuting a claim of right by the particular technique of establishing the facts and the law applicable to them.

This leads on to the question whether in the legal process a legal rule or legal principle has some essential function with regard to the verdict, even though, as we have seen, that essential function (if any) is not to determine the verdict. One might expect to find such an essential function firstly because the process proceeds on the claim of right and secondly because jurists attribute great importance to the correct legal doctrine. In a society where division of labour allows the growth of legal specialists, these specialists devote great energy to finding and expounding the correct doctrine. To say the very least, this expenditure of energy would be excessive if legal rules or principles had no essential function with regard to the decision in the process.

It seems to me that the one and only essential function here of law, or of a legal rule or principle, is to justify or make acceptable, that is to validate, the decision so that in turn the essential function of the legal process is satisfied. (As was stated at the beginning of this chapter, failure of the essential function must not be built into the system, although in individual instances the essential function may fail. An occasional failure of the essential function of the legal process will not make the legal rule any less law but will tend to cause the legal rule to undergo change.) Whether or not in reality the decision in the individual process is reached by applying the appropriate legal rules to the established facts, the verdict will be couched or explained or justified—expressly or impliedly—in terms of law applied to fact.

If this conclusion is correct then it means that the legal rule itself should not appear to be too unjust or too opposed to the interests of a very powerful section of society since otherwise the essential function of the legal process would be frustrated. In addition it means that at the level of the legal process the legal rule must be stable yet flexible and capable of development or the same result will ensue.

But it is clear that to make the legal process acceptable the legal rule need not be the best possible that can be and is envisaged for the society at large or for the ruling élite. The legal rule can perform its essential function perfectly well without being a rule particularly suited to the society in which it operates. And yet, it is when it is exposed to the public view during a legal process that the defects in the rule are at their most obvious. I have argued elsewhere that rules of private law are to a great extent out of step with the needs and desires of society and of its ruling élite, and that the main reason for this state of affairs is inertia.[46] The basic explanation of the inertia is that the essential function of a rule is served whether or not the rule is the best possible provided only that it does not offend too greatly against the ethic or the power base.

If we turn to consider the legal decision, we see that its major virtue is that it should be acceptable, not necessarily that the law be correctly applied to the facts. This can be illuminating both for legal theory—in clarifying the importance of American Legal Realism for instance—and for practice—for example in explaining the continuing popularity of the jury in Britain, especially in criminal trials. It can be a virtue that the jury's verdict is not always that which seems to follow from the facts apparently demonstrated and from the relevant legal rules.

(VI)

If it is reasonable to define something in terms of its essential characteristics and to think of a human institution in terms of what it does—and it is, I believe, reasonable to do both these things—then we may at this stage tentatively offer a definition of laws, only from the narrow viewpoint of the legal process, as:

> Law is the means adopted to institutionalise dispute situations and to validate decisions given in the appropriate process which itself has the specific object of inhibiting further unregulated conflict.

It will emerge from a later chapter whether such a definition can be justified when law is looked at more generally and not just from this one viewpoint. If, as will be maintained, the existence of a process is not only an essential feature but is the sole essential feature of law then it automatically follows that the only essential functions of law are those which it has concerned with the legal process. It should, however, be stressed that just as the essential function of law means the minimum function of law, so this definition, based on the essential function, must be a minimum definition of law. It is worth noting at this point that rules of evidence and procedure fit this definition.

At various points it has been noticed in passing that the functions of a legal process are achieved by means of a decision. The decision is an essential feature of a legal process as here envisaged. A hearing which terminates merely in a recommendation is, in my view, not a legal process. The 'court' must declare 'This is the case' or 'You must do this' whether or not it has any power to enforce its decision directly. A recommendation that admits that the parties have a *right* not to accept it is not enough to count as a legal decision.[47]

We are now in a position to discuss the case of victimless crimes that might be thought to cause difficulties both for the essential function of the legal process as argued above and for the idea of law. In the case of crime where there is a victim it can be said that there is a dispute involving the offender, the victim, the public at large and the state. The process has the specific object of inhibiting further unregulated conflict that might otherwise be caused by criminals being encouraged to further crimes, by victims taking retaliatory action, by fear or tension in the community resulting in violence, or by forcible uncontrolled measures by the state executive. Where the crime does not involve a victim, for example homosexual behaviour between consenting adults, then the picture is radically altered. Can the process be said to inhibit further unregulated conflict? Two situations should be distinguished. In the first and overwhelmingly common situation the behaviour under consideration is regarded as 'disgusting' (especially if it is flaunted) or dangerous by some people in the society; here there would be tension in the community, and the process (to discourage such behaviour) does serve to inhibit unregulated conflict. This situation presents no problem for the views set forth in this book. In the second, the behaviour is socially acceptable, it does not cause disgust, and would not lead to unregulated conflict. For this to be an effective example, the behaviour that is criminal must be such as not to raise the ire of even the government or of the state executive. Such facts can be envisaged only on the assumption that the behaviour is criminal merely because at an earlier period it was thought disgusting or dangerous and that attitudes have changed without the law itself undergoing alteration. Should a prosecution be brought in such circumstances it cannot be said that the trial inhibits unregulated conflict. But the failure here of law or of the legal process is actually different and more fundamental: there is—apart from the law itself—in fact no real dispute, but only an imagined one. In such a case the law is bad law and is liable to be changed. The defect is primarily one of law, only secondarily of the process. Just as bad law may on occasion cause a failure of the essential function of the process by promoting unregulated conflict from the decision, so it can cause a similar failure by creating an unreal dispute where there was no possibility otherwise of unregulated conflict. In neither eventuality is the occasional failure of the essential function built into the process.

Similar in this regard to victimless crime is suicide, when it is treated as criminal. A process might ensue, for example, depriving those who would otherwise be the suicide's heirs from inheriting; or lie against someone whose suicide bid was unsuccessful. Here, too, unless the criminality is a survival, suicide which is regarded as disgusting or dangerous may well cause unregulated conflict, for instance at the graveside. The function of the process, then, is *inter alia* to serve as a deterrent to would-be suicides, thus inhibiting further unregulated conflict.

Finally on the process I should like to call attention to one aspect of very early legal development. It would be accepted by all scholars that in the early days of law legislation does not exist, that law is created by decisions in legal processes sooner than by promulgated laws.[48] But we have seen that for the legal process a first essential function of law is to enable the dispute to be brought before the 'court'. Hence, although the verdict of the 'court' may be the first authoritative statement of the law, we must nonetheless hold that the idea of pertinent law and of a legal claim existed before the judicial utterance.

(VII)

Law in action is also clearly to be seen in juristic acts. A juristic act, for example making a testament or entering a contract of marriage, is a voluntary manifestation of the will where the human will is given legal effectiveness. The term does not include acts where the law binds someone against his will, for instance where there is a general duty not to defame others or negligently damage other people's property, because a juristic act is an act *within* the law. The juristic act is always associated with a social act, and at times there is a tendency not to distinguish the two aspects of the act. Yet it should be stressed that the social act may exist independently of and prior to its being a juristic act: that is, the voluntary manifestation of the human will may exist without the will being given legal effectiveness. For example, A may agree with B to exchange his mare for B's bull, and the parties may put their agreement into effect, or A, but not B, may perform his part of the bargain without there being any legal effectiveness or protection. There may be the social act of barter, and indeed the social institution of barter, without there necessarily being a juristic act of barter. People may exchange goods for goods long before the introduction of a contract applicable to the barter situation. I emphasise this because it is easy to confuse the functions of the social act with the functions of the same act viewed as a juristic act. The function of barter as a social act—basically the exchange between A and B of something that one has and wants less than what the other has and will give in return—is one thing, the legal function of barter as a juristic act—which we will examine in a moment—quite another. Likewise if we were to ask 'What is the function of marriage?' we should be clear whether we are asking about marriage as a social institution or as a legal institution.

A juristic act is nothing more than a social act that has been given legal effectiveness and that is contemplated from the legal angle. The function, then, of the legal effectiveness is to bolster the social act.

When we come to look for the essential function we find two alternative approaches available. We might begin by listing the various possible functions, such as to bolster the social act by doing justice, or to bolster the social act in the best social or political interests of the ruling élite. But this approach is now unnecessarily complicated and we can short-circuit the whole business by observing at once that the legal effectiveness in all cases bolsters the social act by providing means for the resolution of a possible dispute. The means provided are nothing other than the legal process and, since we know the essential function of the legal process, we can say simply: the essential function of the juristic act is to bolster the social act by providing means for the resolution of a possible dispute with the specific object of avoiding further unregulated conflict.

It might be suggested that this short-circuiting has been too drastic, and that one should at least claim that the essential function of the juristic act is to bolster the social act by providing means for the *avoidance* or resolution of a possible dispute with the specific object of avoiding unregulated conflict. This analysis, I suggest, would not be persuasive. One cannot say, for instance, that the essential function of marriage as a juristic act is to avoid possible matrimonial disputes. Also, one could argue that the clear setting out of clauses in a contract so as to avoid disputes is more part of the contract as a social act than as a juristic act; at least, such a clear setting out of the terms is as much needed where the business transaction has no legal effectiveness.

Of course, one extremely important function of the juristic act (or of law in the juristic act and in other areas of possible conflict as well) is to channel behaviour. This channelling is at times to avoid conflict, at times more obviously to obtain a result desired by the society. The force of the argument at this stage may under-emphasise channelling as a legal function. But what has to be stressed here is that channelling in a juristic act (or in other areas governed by law) is achieved because means are provided for the resolution of any possible dispute.[49]

If the analysis of the essential function of the juristic act is correct, then the essential function of the law or legal rules relating to the act will be that which they have with regard to the legal process.

Society's rôle and stake in the juristic act is obscured because that act is primarily a social act made between individuals with society appearing only in the background.

2

The Essence of Law

(I)

The line pursued in the previous chapter inevitably meant that the legal process appeared very prominently in the concept of law and in the provisional definition. It is now time to consider whether the process with its decision is so important for the idea of law, and whether it is indeed essential. We shall first ask whether in a 'primitive society' there can be law without an institutionalised legal process; next whether in a developed system there can be legal rules without an appropriate process; then whether it is the existence of an institutionalised process that distinguishes law from other human situations. This will then bring us to the question whether there is an essential difference between the legal rules of a state and, say, the rules of a religious group or of a trade union. From these investigations we should also learn whether any other element is essential to law—because the process is essential to law (if indeed it is) it would not follow that there are not also other essential elements of law that are unconnected with the process. This will involve considering whether legal rules and legal processes can exist independently of anything that might be described as a legal system.

If it be established, as I believe it will, that the possibility of a process is the essential element of law, we will be led to consider whether the process must also always be the central feature of law. And we must also ask whether the definition of law given in the previous chapter in connection with the process can stand as a general definition of law.

The legal process as it is understood here contains elements revealed in the previous chapter that can be usefully restated: it is called into being by a claim of legal right, power or privilege, it institutionalises a dispute situation, it contains a decision that is validated (expressly or not) by reference to rules, and its essential function is to resolve the dispute with the specific object of inhibiting further unregulated conflict.

(II)

One approach to a definition of a social concept such as law (or religion) is by an enumeration of its essential elements. Boundaries have to be fixed which sharply separate that concept, law, from other concepts. The definition cannot be arbitrary, yet from a historical perspective no definition of such a creation can be wholly satisfactory, since the movement from not-law to law will be gradual, and the characteristic attributes of law will appear only over a period of time. Law does not appear full-fledged from nothing. A human group will come to act in particular ways. At one stage in the history of the group an outsider with experience of other groups might confidently say that the group's rules of behaviour are not law; at another stage the outsider might as confidently state that some of the rules of the group are law. To determine the moment when rules that are not law progress into rules that are law must in some degree be an artificial intellectual activity since the progression will—at least in many cases—be slow, without sudden, drastic changes. Yet to understand the nature of law we must, in fact, draw distinctions and claim that one rule is not law and another is law. The vital thing is that the distinction—though in one sense too sharp—must be drawn at the most appropriate place. And we must accept that there is some such appropriate place. The question for us, therefore, in considering a 'primitive society' is whether we should say that rules hallowed by custom or accepted morality become law at the precise point when dispute situations are institutionalised and when a process comes into existence whose decisions are validated in order to avoid further unregulated conflict. There are, I think, two main arguments for making such an assertion. The first is that no other point is anything like so suitable for marking the progression; the institutionalisation of disputes and the establishment of a process for reaching and validating decisions is a crucial point in human thinking that has no rival in the transition from custom to law.

The force of this argument (and indeed, as we shall see, of

the second argument also) becomes apparent when we look at what alone might be suggested as an alternative moment for dating the transformation of custom into law, namely the point at which decisions, however reached, will either be enforced by some machinery external to the parties or at which the losing party will suffer some regulated sanction[1] imposed upon him by persons other than his opponent. In other words, on this view the decisive moment would be when the victorious party need not rely simply on self-help and undefined social pressure to enforce a judgement against a recalcitrant loser. Where the process allows us to distinguish between plaintiff and defendant the important case here would, of course, be where the defendant is the loser. Now, in the history of a legal system the stage at which decisions can be enforced against a losing defendant is one of great importance, but it cannot be used, I think, as the touchstone for determining the transition from custom to law. The reason is that it may well—and in fact on occasion does—occur far too late. On that basis International law would still not be law. Nor would Roman private law of the Republican and classical periods be law since, as J. M. Kelly has shown,[2] litigation was then devoid of the sanction of state powers, despite the formidable array of legislation, juristic opinion, discussion and writings, and courts. And whereas some scholars might claim that International law is not law, it has never been suggested that Rome of the Republic and Empire was a society untrammelled by private law. The point of development at which a judgement can be enforced naturally often coincides with the point at which a defendant can be compelled to accept the jurisdiction of the 'court'. (In the case of what we would term 'criminal law' intervention of the state powers may be earlier than in the case of 'private law'.)

The second argument is that the point at which dispute situations are institutionalised provides us with a test for marking law off from custom and morality, which does correspond better than do other tests with general ideas as to what law is. Although it is unlikely that there can ever be complete agreement as to what is to be included or not included within the scope of a social concept, this must not prevent us from trying to analyse the scope of the concept and its fundamental features. What is important is that the scope attributed to a concept for analytical purposes should coincide with general ideas as to its range. 'General ideas' on the range of a social concept are to be discovered primarily, and most easily, by linguistic usage. The word 'law' is, of course, used with a variety of meanings. Above all, its sense in a phrase such as 'the laws of chemistry' is very different from what we have been discussing. The laws of chemistry concern physical properties; the laws with which we are concerned are norms. But the sense of the term 'law' when used of primitive law and International law is not usually considered to be different *in kind* from its sense in 'welfare law', 'Scots law', 'public law'.

In discussing the transition—as well as in other contexts—I have tried to avoid using the word 'court' and to talk instead of the 'institutionalising of dispute situations' and of a 'process'. The reason is that to a Western jurist the word 'court' conjures up a picture of a body formally constituted, which meets regularly in a fixed place or places. By 'institutionalising' and 'process' I have in mind something that may be far less formal. Just on the border-line on its way into law I would place the situation recorded by Franz Boas and related by E. A. Hoebel.[3] An Eskimo named Padlu, who was a native of Padli, killed on three separate occasions. A headman asked every man in Padli whether Padlu should be killed. An affirmative answer was obtained from all and the headman on a hunting trip shot Padlu in the back. If it were habitual with Eskimos to deal with recidivist killers in this way, then the practice may be thought to be sufficiently institutionalised and sufficiently a process for it to be law. But if this were not a habitual way for Eskimos to treat the situation then it would certainly not be law: it would not be sufficiently institutionalised, and it is this institutionalising that makes the headman's questioning of all the men, their answer and his subsequent behaviour into a process. We may choose as a clear example of a process another instance adduced by Hoebel,[4] this time from the Yurok Indians of California.

> An aggrieved Yurok who felt he had a legitimate claim engaged the legal services of two nonrelatives from a community other than his own. The defendant then did likewise. These men were called 'crossers'; they crossed back and forth between the litigants. The principals to the dispute did not ordinarily face each other during the course

> of the action. After hearing all that each side had to offer in evidence and pleading as to the relevant substantive law, the crossers rendered a decision for damages according to a well-established scale that was known to all. For their footwork and efforts each received a piece of shell currency called a 'moccasin'.

On the approach I have suggested (as well as that of Hoebel) there is no doubt that here we have law with the institutionalising of a dispute and a recognisable process. Later in this chapter, I shall attempt to determine what precisely are the minimum requirements of an institutionalised process.

(III)

To the question whether in a developed legal system there can be legal rules without an appropriate process there is a simple answer in the negative. It is, of course, true that statutes frequently do not set out the law in terms of the process—a statute, for example, may do nothing more than define legal terms. But revealing as this fact may be for the nature of legislation it tells us little about the nature of law or of legal rules. The significant thing for us at the moment is simply that in a developed system a legal rule is unthinkable unless it can be used to bring a dispute situation into the context of a process and/or validate the decision. The process, of course, may be a court or an administrative tribunal or it may involve the services of an arbiter who is selected by some accepted mechanism.

Again, in the modern state much legislation can best be described as regulatory: for example statutes introducing and organising a national health service, determining the circumstances in which social security benefits are payable, and nationalising industries. In all such legislation the idea of a process does not appear to be prominent. Yet the possibility of a process is there, of course, and if a dispute arose the norms set out in these laws would appropriately be used both to initiate the process and to validate any decision given in the process. Such regulatory statutes really pose the different problem, which will be discussed later in the chapter, namely does the process always have to be the central feature of law?

The importance of courts for the nature of law in the

developed modern state has already been emphasised by Sir John Salmond. In the seventh edition of his *Jurisprudence*[5] (the last that he edited himself) he claimed

> But all law, however made, is recognized and administered by the Courts, and no rules are recognized and administered by the Courts which are not rules of law. It is therefore to the Courts and not the legislature that we must go to ascertain the true nature of law. The law may be defined as the body of principles recognised and applied by the state in the administration of justice. In other words, the law consists of the rules recognised and acted on by courts of justice.

It has been argued, properly in my view, that this definition is too narrow even for the law of a modern state. Thus the present editor of Salmond's *Jurisprudence*, P. J. Fitzgerald, asks:[6] if a commissioner under the National Insurance Act, 1956, lays down a rule that he intends to follow in exercising his discretion, is this law? He further observes that other persons and bodies besides law courts and administrators enforce rules of conduct and he instances imprisonment by order of the House of Commons for breaches of privilege; and he also claims that Salmond's definition is not appropriate to statute-law, which is law as soon as it is passed and does not have to wait for recognition by the courts. But telling though these objections may be against Salmond, they do not adversely affect a definition of law that is in terms of the means to institutionalise disputes and validate decisions given in the relevant process. As with primitive law, so with modern state law the idea of 'institutionalised process' is wider than the notion of 'court'.

(IV)

The process and the institutionalising of disputes do seem, moreover, to distinguish law sharply from other human situations. In this way we can distinguish rules of law from the precepts of morality. Although a social sanction may follow upon a breach of morals just as upon the breaking of a law, a breach of morals that does not also involve breaking a law will not give rise to anything that can be characterised as a regular process. Again, the problem, which so delights the Positivists, of the gunman who can enforce his command with a sanction poses no difficulties for us: his command is not law since it is not backed by an institutionalised process. This present emphasis should not be taken as implying that all interesting and typically legal phenomena are exclusively concerned with the process, but only that phenomena which cannot lead to a process and the institutionalised resolution of a dispute are not legal.

But what our definition of law does not do is distinguish the laws of a state from the rules of some other human group, even of a self-constituted group. Thus, if a group of worshippers were to found their own minority Church and draft rules for it and for the behaviour of the members and set out a procedure for deciding disputes, the rules would be law within the terms of our definition. Even if we allow that a dissident member called to appear before the appropriate tribunal might refuse to acknowledge its authority and might abandon his membership of the Church, and that no way might exist of enforcing a decision against him, this would not—for us—alter the status of the rules as law, since I have claimed that law may exist even where the defendant cannot be compelled to concede the jurisdiction of the 'court' and even where there is no regulated method of enforcing a judgement. By similar reasoning the rules of a trade union, which institutionalise disputes and validate decisions given in the process fixed for the union, are rules of law. On the view proposed here, such rules of a group are law and, as law, are not essentially different from the law of a state. We must, however, be clear as to what is meant by a group. For our purposes the opinion of A. M. Honoré is satisfactory: 'a group may be described as a collection of individuals who share a fairly definite understanding of what is to be done by one or more of themselves in given circumstances, or how the question what is to be done in these circumstances is to be decided. "What is to be done" here includes "What is not to be done" and "What may be done".'[7]

The conclusion that the rules of a group may be law is not new and has recently also been reached through a different route by Honoré who insists that the explanation of the special status of the laws of territorial states must be sought elsewhere than in their systematic character or in the existence of special institutions to identify them. This explanation he finds in the intimate connection between law and obedience since, he says, in a conflict a special pre-eminence will naturally attach to the laws of the group that is in a position to compel other groups to conform to its prescription, and in the modern world the territorial group will be in this powerful position vis-à-vis private associations, religious and political movements, and professional bodies.[8] A rather different explanation in terms of the essential function of the process will be given in the next section of this chapter, and it, I believe, is logically satisfactory. But the pre-eminence of the law of territorial states is also partly a psychological matter and here one must add to Honoré's account. Law has attributes that are not essential but are typical; thus, law claims to be authoritative, the rules are part of a system, the system claims jurisdiction in a wide range of matters, the rules elicit obedience, and the rules are or derive from a sovereign's command. The more legal rules partake of these typical attributes, the more law-like the rules become. Laws of a territorial state have more of these attributes and have them more markedly than have, for instance, the rules of International law or of a trade union. Hence the law of a territorial state is law *par excellence*. The typical attributes of law are the subject of the next chapter.

To be distinguished from a process are some forms of arbitration. All arbitration involves the institutionalising of disputes and much arbitration does involve a process complete with a decision. But in some arbitration the tribunal cannot issue a decision and can only make a recommendation to the parties in dispute. Such arbitration, in my view, cannot amount to a legal process, and is not based on a legal claim, nor in the nature of things can law validate the decision. No more need be said at this stage; further elucidation of the distinction between such arbitration and the legal process will be found at the end of the next chapter.

(V)

The recognition that the rules of a group can be law does, however, raise a problem that must be resolved: are all group rules that can give rise to a process to be regarded as law? If not, on what does the status of a rule as law depend? The difficulty is plain to see, I think, if we consider the activity of an illegal revolutionary group. Let us take two cases. First, a revolutionary group that is in *de facto* control of part of a State's territory declares that particular conduct will be treated as constituting an offence and be punishable. A member of the group is said to have offended against the declaration, is tried by a tribunal, found guilty and punished. Is this an example of law and legal process ? There is a dispute that has been institutionalised, and there has been a process that has validated the decision, and the object has been to inhibit further unregulated conflict. Ordinary linguistic usage, moreover, could in this case talk of law and legal process. Secondly, an urban guerilla group that has effective control over no territory announces that it will try and will execute capitalists. The revolutionaries seize a businessman who is not a member of the group, establish by investigation that he is wealthy and is an employer of labour, and shoot him. It is not easy to use the terms 'law' and 'legal process' in this latter case, and there would generally be, I believe, great reluctance to admit that true law is involved in the second example. But where does the difference lie between real law and non-law such as appears clearly in this second example ?

The difference does not lie in the form; but this must not distress us. In a case such as has been described, when it would be wrong to talk of law, the non-law is in fact 'mock law'. It is non-law that is claiming to be law, demanding to be treated as law, mimicking law, and deliberately taking the appearance of law. Without the notion of real law, this mock law could not exist.

The answer is to be sought in the area of a claim made earlier in this book that the recognised practices must be acceptable, which entails, I declared, that rules come into existence by an approved method. 'For a method to be approved it must rest somehow on authority that is recognised as such, and obeyed as such.' The ideas of authority and acceptability are inextricably bound together, although one or the other may appear more vividly in a given situation. To clarify the notions I should like to look first at examples where the answer to the question 'Law or not law' is in my view self-evident. To begin with an instance of delegated legislation. Let us imagine that (in a time of stability) a supreme legislature gives power to a subordinate body to make binding rules on a particular topic. The subordinate body issues what purports to be legislation on a totally different matter not entrusted to it. Here it is clear that the subordinate legislation is not true law; it is *ultra vires*. That is to say, it is a rule that ought not to be accepted by those in charge of a dispute-resolving process, on the assumption that they accept the enabling law as limiting the delegated power. The reason is that in a complex society where law-making bodies are arranged hierarchically, the validity of law made by a subordinate body depends on the authority granted for that purpose by a higher body. A second very different example would be where a citizen charged with a nasty crime, which he had committed for his own selfish non-political ends, declares that he does not recognise the authority of the court to try him. In this instance, it is equally self-evident that the status of the trial as a legal process, and of the relevant rules as law, is not affected by the party's claim. The authority of the law or legal process does not depend on its being acceptable to or accepted by everyone, or even by those directly concerned. For a third, slightly more doubtful example let us consider the case of a lawfully constituted trade union that passes a resolution contrary to the ordinary law of the land. The resolution would not be law in my view because it is in direct conflict with more powerful law; hence it is not acceptable and has not sufficient authority. Because of its conflict with more powerful law, the union's rule cannot resolve disputes.

The principle would seem to be that when a group makes a rule that goes against law made by a body with greater power or authority[9] the group's rule is not law, either because it cannot resolve a dispute (since the decision can be set aside) or because where it might be said to resolve a particular dispute (for instance, by actually executing someone who had been seized) the resultant conflict with the higher authority means that the dispute was not settled with the specific object of inhibiting further unregulated conflict.

Before leaving this section let us return to the lawful trade union that passes a resolution contrary to the ordinary law of the land and that conducts processes conforming to the terms of the resolution. If we suppose that in this regard the union is more powerful than the government, that the state will not enforce the ordinary law of the land, and that no action will lie which could bring it about that the ordinary law of the land would prevail, then we should concede that the union resolution is law.

(VI)

The extension of the idea of law to include the rules of a group, coupled with the view that an essential feature of law is the institutionalised process, means that it is critical for us to determine what amounts to such a process. Examples have already been given to indicate what may count as a process for primitive law. With regard to a group within a state, a crucial case, I suggest, is that of a family. That a family does or may comprise a group as defined above is apparent. But can, or do, decisions within a family amount to an institutionalised process? The answer is that sometimes they do, but usually they do not.

One example of the former alternative is sufficient. In Rome of the Kings, the Republic and even into the Empire, the head of a family had power of life, of death and of lesser punishment over even the grown up members of the family. It seems that the XII Tables, a legal code of the fifth century B.C., conceded the right of a father to put a son to death only 'on just cause'. The right to punish belonged to the father. Yet in practice it seems that he summoned a family council (which would include friends as well as actual relatives), which sat in judgement with him, and he accepted their decision by majority vote. This family council apparently had no standing within the law of the state, yet the father's use of it would protect him from a charge of acting arbitrarily. The hearing of such a family council si sufficiently institutionalised—though outside of the law or legal structure of the state—to be regarded as a process.[10]

A family decision that is not sufficiently institutionalised is, however, much easier to visualise. Thus, two boys squabble over an apple, each claiming that it is his, and the one who does not have it in his hand appeals to his mother. She listens to the competing claims and decides who has right to the apple. The appeal to the mother, her hearing of the claim and the decision are not sufficiently institutionalised to be a process. Ordinary language, indeed, would exclude the use of the word 'process' here except in mock-heroic terms. But where does the difference lie between this and the preceding example?

The difference is one of degree, not of kind. Just as among 'primitive people' no strict dividing line can be drawn factually between what is not a process and what is a process, but a stage of development can be visualised where there is no process, and a slightly later stage where behaviour in a dispute situation can reasonably be described as an institutionalised process, so within the family. But the societal structure that is a 'primitive' community is in general much more complex than the structure of a Western family. Hence the methods adopted to resolve disputes are institutionalised much more often in a 'primitive' society than in a family. It is thus natural to consider the methods of dispute-solving among a 'primitive' people as amounting to a process but very difficult to call dispute-solving within a family a process.

Although there is no acid-test for distinguishing a process from dispute-solving without a process, one can point to certain indicators that are typical of a process. Thus, a process will tend to have some formalities, there will be some regularity in handling dispute situations, there will be an absence of total arbitrariness from the procedure or from the decision or from both, and those involved in a process—in addition to the disputing parties who are usually in earnest—will treat the dispute-solving with an air of seriousness. Wittgenstein's idea of 'family likeness' is relevant here.

In this section, to avoid a circular argument, I have tried to explain 'process' without involving the idea of law. But if the arguments earlier in the chapter have validity then necessarily we have to regard the family council of early Rome as being concerned with matters of law. In the next chapter it will be argued that such law would be low-level law.

(VII)

That the process (or the possibility of the process) is an essential feature of law does not by itself necessarily mean that the process is the sole essential feature of law. But it seems impossible to find any other feature that can be regarded as essential. Thus, we have already seen that a regulated sanction cannot be considered as essential; likewise law does not always arise from the command of a political superior.

It is frequently assumed that a law or legal rule must be part of a legal system, and if this were so then this would be another essential feature of law.[11] Now exactly what is meant by a legal system is a matter that will have to be considered shortly. At the moment all that need be said is that one legal rule with its appropriate process cannot be regarded as forming a system. Yet, one can easily envisage a 'primitive society', such as Eskimos, with only one legal rule and only one process, namely that concerned with recidivist killing. In the long historical development towards law and legal system it would surely be wrong to deny the title of law to individual rules that become institutionalised simply because the structure is not yet so developed as to constitute a system.

(VIII)

If I may sum up the main argument to this point: the essential feature of a law or legal rule is the existence of an appropriate institutionalised process, and this is the sole essential feature of law. The essential function of this process is to resolve actual or potential disputes with the specific object of inhibiting further unregulated conflict. In the context of the process a claim of legal right or power or privilege is essential to call the process into being and legal rules must validate the decision.

It might be objected that this approach makes it excessively difficult to recognise law when we see it. This at the most would be a practical and not a theoretical problem; but in any event the difficulty can be exaggerated. There is no great difficulty in recognising a process when one exists. The difficulty is rather when the process of a group cannot be regarded as a legal process because it fails in the specific object of such a process since it is in conflict with the law of a more powerful group. But the practical difficulty here can scarcely be greater than that experienced under Hans Kelsen's famous 'Pure Theory of Law': according to this, law is a hierarchy of norms, the validity of each of which derives from another norm that stands behind it and so on until we reach the initial, fundamental norm, the Grundnorm, which has no rule behind it and which imparts validity to the whole constitution.[12]

It seems, therefore, that we can still accept the minimum

definition of law proposed in the previous chapter, namely:

> Law is the means adopted to institutionalise disputes and to validate decisions given in the appropriate process that has the specific object of inhibiting further unregulated conflict.

If this definition contains all the essentials and nothing but the essentials, it might seem to follow that law and the legal process are about order—if I may use the word 'order' loosely for the moment. This is self-evident for the process. If the process is the sole essential feature of law—and it seems to be—then the sole essential functions of law are those it has with regard to the process. Hence it might be argued that the prime purpose of law is to make, preserve and restore order, and that it also follows that this purpose of law is an end in itself. For law to be law, to fulfil the prime function of law on this argument, it would be sufficient for it to make, preserve or restore order. One need not go on to say—indeed one could not say—that law reaches order in the inevitable interest of something else such as liberty or justice. The argument to this point, however, if not positively wrong, is at least too elliptical. One should not attribute directly to law the essential function of the process. Admittedly, if the process is the sole essential feature of law, the only functions that are essential to law are those it has with respect to the process. But these essential functions are to institutionalise dispute situations and to validate decisions given in the process. More importantly, the function of the process 'to inhibit further unregulated conflict' can refer only to the period of time after the process. But the law existed or was at least inchoate before the process, and one cannot directly transfer the function 'to inhibit further unregulated conflict' from the time after the process to the time before the process. An example will make plain what is meant. Imagine that a statute introduces for the first time unemployment benefits. Should a dispute arise whether a particular person is entitled to benefit, a process will resolve the dispute, and the process will have the specific object of inhibiting further unregulated conflict. But before the statute was passed, there was no right to benefit, hence no dispute situation and no unregulated conflict to be inhibited unless, which need not be the case, the statute was the response to conflict. Indeed, law creates legal rights. The feeling that one's legal rights have been infringed may cause the conflict. Yet law provides the process and by doing so demonstrates the intention of regulating future conflict. The law itself may create the possibility of the dispute situation but it does and must provide the means for resolving the dispute with, indeed, the specific object of inhibiting further unregulated conflict. What law is essentially about, that is to say, is not the reduction or elimination of dispute situations or actual disputes but the machinery for institutionalising these and thus inhibiting *unregulated* conflict. Thus, statute may create a new legal right, say, again, to unemployment benefits. Such a right is logically prior to any process, and the creation of the right is primarily in order to confer an economic advantage, not to give rise to or even resolve disputes. Nonetheless, rights of this kind are not to be seen isolated from the process. True, the intention behind the creation of the right is the conferment of economic advantage, but what makes the right in question a legal right and not some other kind of right is precisely the availability of a process to resolve any dispute that may arise.

If, with regard to usages regulating the public relations of individuals to the state or group and the public conduct of members or sections of the community to each other, we treat the term 'order' as signifying that however many disputes there may be they can be institutionalised so that unregulated conflict is inhibited, and that turbulence and unruliness are restrained, then law is basically about order. It will be convenient to use 'disorder' in the converse sense to that attributed to order.

Law, of course, is frequently used to channel behaviour and to implement a policy decision that activity should be directed along specific lines. A government, especially in a totalitarian régime, may for ideological reasons promulgate a statute that will lead—as, perhaps, the government knows—to violent conflict. Here, one may say that law itself produces unregulated conflict. But one must stress first the process and second the force that backs the law and is an integral part of it (and which is treated in chapter 5). Directly it is the legal process whose essential function includes the specific object of inhibiting further unregulated conflict. Unless this object, at least in the moderate long term, is achieved, then the law and the legal rule will have collapsed. Law may be used to create change, a different social structure from that already in existence. And in the course of changing one social structure for another it may well produce unregulated conflict, disorder. But this disorder ought to be purely temporary. If it is not, then it would, I believe, be generally agreed that the law is a failure (whether or not the régime survives). And if law that is productive of continuing disorder must be deemed a failure then it must still follow that law is fundamentally about order.

The basic function of law is, therefore, order, which is an end in itself. Law may, and at times certainly does, have an end beyond order, but this end, however desirable it might be, is subordinate to order. If one considers justice, liberty, the channelling of social behaviour, in terms of functions of law then one has to say that they are necessary to law only in so far as their absence would cause a failure of this essential function of order. Consequent upon this, the greatest failing—and there can be failures—of an individual legal rule or process, considered as law, is that it causes rather than inhibits disorder. The success or failure of a legal rule or process is, of course, not to be measured by the immediate response to it, but by the effects in the long term.

In this sense law reflects society. Justice and freedom are preserved by law to no less and no greater an extent than the society as structured requires and permits: that is, in addition to its function with regard to order, what law does or can do depends on the society in which it operates and not on any intrinsic qualities of law. Thus, if a particular society had no concern for justice in some matters, a lack of justice in the relevant rules and processes would have no deleterious effect on the efficacy or status of the law. But if a society cared passionately about justice, legal rules and processes would have to be just to avoid a failure of the essential functions relating to order.

Yet, possibly paradoxically, law is not seen by legislators or legal interpreters or even by non-lawyers as being, in the main, solely concerned with order. A law maker does not say 'We need some rule and it does not matter whether it gives solution A or B. Let it be B'; rather the claim is 'We must have solution B because it protects the best interests of the community'. Typically, law is seen as being for justice, freedom, the regulation of society, while nonetheless involving order. James Lorimer, the famous

Edinburgh natural lawyer of a century ago puts this position beautifully, in a passage that, also for another reason, deserves to be quoted *in extenso*:

> But the conditions under which our rights are realized, rather than the origin of these rights, or the final end of their exercise, being the subjects with which jurisprudence, when seen not as a science but as an art, is mainly conversant,—the realization of order, and not the attainment of liberty, came very generally to be regarded as the final and exclusive object of jurisprudence. The error, like most errors, was a half-truth; for the condition—the means which was thus mistaken for the end—being not one of many conditions or means, but the condition *sine qua non*, the exclusive and infallible means—the means without which its attainment was inevitable—this means, if not identical with the end, was involved in it, and in the last analysis implied in it. If you analyse liberty you will find order, just as if you analyse order you will find liberty. Perfect order is liberty; perfect liberty is order. But the practical results of the error have not been on this account less fatal; for it has been by considering order as an end in itself, and by forgetting that its value ceases the moment that it fails to fulfil the function of a means towards the attainment of liberty, that authority has been hardened into despotism, that obedience has degenerated into slavery, that nation has been separated from nation, class from class, and man from man, till humanity itself has groaned under the burden which was bound on its back by honest and upright, but ignorant hands. The principle that the perfection of legislative, as of all other machinery, consists in its simplicity, and that so soon as a law becomes needless it becomes injurious,—a stumbling-stone in the way to liberty, an impediment in our progress towards the realization of the final end of life,—was the great discovery of the eighteenth century.[13]

The question of law as it is in human societies and how it ought to be when determined by nature will be touched on in a later chapter. We may, however, note one element of great significance in this passage. In our terms Lorimer is saying in effect that law is fundamentally about order. But in his own terms he is bound to go further, and he equates order with liberty. This seems violently paradoxical and can be explained only in terms of some philosophy, namely Hegelian. From our viewpoint, Lorimer's equalization of the two seems explicable only on a conflation of positive law and natural law: that is to say, the essential function of positive law appears to be order; the essential function of natural law is liberty; but positive law (for Lorimer) is not true law if it conflicts with natural law, hence (the argument should go), order must be the means towards an end, which is liberty.

(IX)

When looking at law from the viewpoint of the process I maintained that a claim of law, a legal rule, was essential to bring the process into being, and that within the process law had the further essential function of validating the decision. The process has emerged as the sole essential feature of law. Accordingly it could be stated in passing that the essential functions of law 'are to institutionalise dispute situations and to validate decisions in the process'. To leave that statement without elaboration could be misleading. It cannot be taken to mean—as it might appear to mean—that it is an essential of law in the event of a dispute to make a process inevitable or even likely to occur. This is easily demonstrated. Thus, many of the most satisfactory legal rules are so drafted that when a dispute arises their very high quality and clarity will ensure that a good result will ensue without recourse to a process. The existence of good legal rules can in practice actually reduce the frequency of processes. It is thus not even necessarily desirable that legal rules lead to the resolving of disputes by bringing about a process. The sense of our statement is that it is an essential function of law to provide the means by which a dispute can be resolved in a process.

This involves us in holding that although the process is both the distinguishing and the essential feature of law it cannot be considered the central feature of law. Many legal disputes are resolved without recourse to a process, much legislation is primarily regulatory in character, and the process is not necessarily prominent. What, however, is central to law is that recourse *can* be had to an appropriate process. The possibility or the threat of a process is the central feature of law.

The possibility of a process affects all legal dealings. For instance, in the case of an agreement to be made between two firms, it will induce them first to make a contract that is legally binding, then to abide by it or deviate from it only with the approval of the other party, and then, if a problem does arise, to try to solve it amicably, fairly, and without undue pressure on one side. The outcome of previous processes, moreover, will indicate to the firms the consequences they might expect to follow from their dealings if a dispute goes to trial, and accordingly this will affect their conduct. It should be stressed that legal rules backed by the possibility of a process provide a feeling of positive security and regulate behaviour, and hence are directly conducive to order.

(X)

An approach to law of the kind I have been suggesting, since it is concerned solely with man-made law, is very different from that of Natural Law. Thus, the approach avoids the possibility of confusion between what the law is and what it ought to be. From the Marxist approach and from that of others who believe in Law as Social Control it differs primarily in insisting that legal rules and processes need correspond only negatively and not also positively to social, economic and political conditions—much inefficient law can be, and is, tolerated, and is satisfactory only in the sense that it provides or maintains some order. I believe that this view of law corresponds much more to general experience.

The approach is positivist but differs from Austinian Positivism in shifting the emphasis from the command of a sovereign to the process. It avoids the artificiality inherent in some of the searches for a command (and sovereign), and at the same time enables the idea of what is law to be widened. More importantly, it focuses attention on law as a dispute-resolving and disorder-inhibiting mechanism, and this is the central feature of law.

The significance of this switch of emphasis should be stressed. Natural Law theories insist that law is made by a superior whether this is God (or a god) or Reason and it is this creation that makes law law. In Christian theory—and not only there—this superior is even to be regarded as a political superior, a sovereign. Natural Law theories of the Age of Reason secularise this approach, retaining the emphasis on the creation of law by a superior. Jeremy Bentham follows on, claiming that the source of a law must be 'the will of a sovereign in *a* state',[14] and Austin is obviously in the same tradition. So indeed in his turn is Kelsen, with his insistence on law as a system of hierarchically arranged norms with a *Grundnorm* as the original or basic norm.

3

The Typical Attributes of Law and Legal Process

(I)

Discussion of the essentials of law and the legal process provides little indication of the richness of the idea of law. In addition to these essential feaures, law and the legal process are distinguished by many other attributes, some of which—though not essential—may be designated as typical and may play a vital rôle in our understanding of and our attitude to law.

But in looking for what is typical we are faced with a problem that must be made express, namely that what is typical in a human institution is obviously not independent of time or place. A similar problem, as has been noted in passing, does also exist in isolating the essential elements of a concept. A concept has no physical existence, hence our view of what are its essential features, what is contained within it or is excluded from it, will depend on what we regard as the limits of the concept. The dangers of circular argument and of subjectivity are inherent in any attempt to determine the essentials of a concept. But the problem is much more acute when we try to decide what is typical. A minimum definition of law can be given that would include certain Eskimo behaviour, but no amount of argument or reasoning would persuade a modern Western lawyer that Eskimo law is typical law. To the Eskimo, on the other hand, what we do would not be typical. It should be understood, therefore, that in discussing the typical attributes of law we are concerned with what appears to be typical to the traditional Western jurist.

On this basis the most important of the typical attributes of law and the legal process are that they form part of a system that is more or less all-embracing, they are created by a recognisable person or body that has the power to make law, they are authoritative and authoritarian, they are backed by regulated sanctions, and they receive obedience.

(II)

The nature of a legal system is well indicated by Hans Kelsen, who claims: 'All norms whose validity may be traced back to one and the same basic norm form a system of norms, or an order. This basic norm constitutes, as a common source, the bond between all the different norms of which an order consists.'[1] So closely linked is law with a legal system that a distinguished legal philosopher, Joseph Raz, can begin a book: 'This work is an introduction to a general study of legal systems, that is to the study of the systematic nature of law, and the examination of the presuppositions and implications underlying the fact that every law necessarily belongs to a legal system (the English, or German, or Roman, or Canon law, or some other system).'[2] As A. M. Honoré says of this statement, Raz 'clearly feels the "fact" he asserts is unproblematic. There is no need to justify the assertion that laws necessarily belong to systems of laws. Nor even is there cause to explain the meaning of the term "system".'[3] This attitude of Raz—and it would be widely shared—is very revealing for the importance of the idea of a system for the notion of law. And yet it does not seem to be wholly accurate. It was argued above that some societies, for example an Eskimo group, might have only one legal rule. That rule can properly be regarded as law, but it is difficult to imagine it forming or being part of a legal system. Nonetheless, we must accept that, typically, a legal rule is part of a legal system.

Raz[4] lists the features that characterise legal systems; legal systems are comprehensive, they claim to be supreme, and they are open systems in the sense that they contain norms whose purpose is to give binding force to norms that are not part of the legal system, hence they maintain and support other forms of social grouping. Of these features the first is by far the most important and alone will be discussed at this stage.[5]

Raz explains what he means by the statement that legal systems are comprehensive in terms that most scholars would find generally acceptable. Legal systems, he says, claim authority to regulate any type of behaviour, and in this differ from most other institutionalised systems. Sport associations, commercial companies, cultural organisations, political parties, and so on, he points out, are all established to achieve certain limited goals and each claims authority over behaviour relevant to that goal only. In his opinion legal systems are different in that they do not acknowledge any limitation of the spheres they claim authority to regulate.

Now this feature is more readily apparent in some legal systems than in others. It is most obvious in the law of a territorial state. A state claims authority over all the behaviour of persons, citizens and non-citizens, within its territory and over all property situated within its territory, and even, in many instances, over the behaviour of its citizens outwith its territory and over property outside its boundaries that belongs to a citizen. The feature is less obvious in some systems of religious law. Thus, Canon law, which Raz expressly admits as a system, was always prepared to accept, both in the Middle Ages and today, that much behaviour—notably that pertaining to the transfer of ownership, to individual contracts and to delict—was largely outwith its authority, and that in these matters the temporal power had authority. Even less obvious is this feature in International law, which traditionally claims authority over relations between states and a very few other matters such as piracy. Admittedly, however, International law has recently, in rather more types of cases claimed authority over international companies and jurisdiction even in some disputes between a state and its nationals. Again, the European Economic Community expressly accepts that its law has authority in respect of certain matters, though not in respect of others, and yet it would be generally thought that Community law forms a legal system.

When we come to consider the rules of trade unions, sports associations, and so on, the typical feature of a legal system of claiming authority to regulate any type of behaviour just does not exist. Yet I have maintained in the previous chapter that the rules of such bodies can be law,[6] and if this is correct we are faced with a choice between three possibilities. It might be suggested (1) that in so far as they are law these group rules form a separate legal system, or (2) that in so far as the rules are law they form part of the legal system of the territorial state, or (3) the rules may be law but neither constitute nor are part of a legal system. Possibility 3 should at once be excluded in view of the definition of a system adopted from Kelsen. The group rules are norms that derive from the group's constitution, which is either the Grundnorm or a norm whose validity is itself to be traced further back to the state's constitution, which will be the Grundnorm. As for the other possibilities, it can at times be the case that the rules of a group are part of the legal system of a territorial state, but this is not always so. If the rules of a group inside a state are neither approved nor disapproved by the state, if a process under the group's rules is not directed or controlled by the state or any of its subordinate divisions, if a judgement in the process is neither recognised nor enforced by the state, then the rules cannot be regarded as part of the law or legal system of the territorial state. Thus it happens that the legal rules of a group can constitute a separate legal system albeit this system lacks the feature of claiming authority over all the behaviour of the members of the group.

If we now return to the proposition that legal rules typically belong to a legal system and that the prime characteristic of a legal system is that it claims authority to regulate any type of behaviour, then in this regard some legal rules are more law-like than others. If this proposition were treated as the sole criterion of 'lawness' then the law of a territorial state would be more law than Canon law, and in further descending order would come International law and some forms of primitive law. The rules of a trade union or other similar body could appear to form a legal system, but not one with the prime characteristic of a legal system. Other forms of primitive law are not part of a legal system, and on this basis would not count as law at all.

(III)

A second typical feature of law is that it is created by a recognisable person or body that has the power to make law. Indeed, John Austin, whose work was seminal for the Positivist theory of law that is still dominant in the English-speaking world, defined law as the general commands of a sovereign, supported by the threat of sanctions. 'Every positive law', he says, 'or every law simply and strictly so called, is set by a sovereign person, or a sovereign body of persons, to a member or members of the independent political society wherein that person or body is sovereign or supreme.'[7] For Austin this sovereign in the United Kingdom, for instance, was 'the king and the peers, with the electoral body of the commons.' Now objections can be and have been levelled against the Austinian theory of law.[8] That fact does not concern us at the moment. What matters here is that, since the theory could attract so much attention and support and is still so influential, we must at least accept that within the Western tradition a typical attribute of law is that it is created by a recognisable person or body with the power to make law. On this approach many norms or systems of norms would fall outside the notion of law. This is notably the case with International law and much of primitive law. We cannot really find a legislature or a sovereign for International law that is largely based on custom.[9] Indeed, Austin expressly denied that International law was law 'properly so called' and he would count it rather as 'positive morality', which might be considered without regard to its goodness or badness as the subject of a science closely analogous to jurisprudence.[10] The most distinguished living Positivist, H.L.A.Hart, declares that primitive law and International law are doubtful cases of law. As he says, 'International law lacks a legislature, states cannot be brought before international courts without their prior consent and there is no centrally organised effective system of sanctions.'[11]

If we take as a criterion of law that it is made by a recognisable person or body with the power to make law then the law of a territorial state is very much law, International law and much primitive law only doubtfully so. Trade union rules and those of many other organizations would rank high on the scale of law.

But even within one system some rules would be more law-like than others. For instance, in the modern Western world some rules still develop from custom, which comes to be accepted as law by the courts of the territorial state. It is not possible to point here to a person or body who made the customary rules.[12]

(IV)

A further typical attribute of law and its related process is that they are authoritarian and authoritative. By authoritarian in this context I mean that those in charge of the law and the process claim authority on that account over the behaviour of the parties to the dispute and assert that the parties must assent to the decision reached in the process and abide by it. By authoritative I mean that those in charge of the law and the process insist that no other body has the right to claim authority over the behaviour of the parties, and that their legal decision is correct because it is their decision.

An example from criminal law will make plain what is meant. John assaults Terry in a city street. The state will claim that it has the right to investigate the assault, summon John before its court even against his will, determine whether what it regards as an assault has taken place, and impose a punishment upon John, however reluctant he may be to receive it. The state will deny a similar right to any other body or person including Terry, and should Terry retaliate by attacking John, the state would claim the right to punish Terry.

So important to law is the attribute of being authoritarian and authoritative that without some trace of it in a given situation there could be no legal process. If persons summoned to court not only could ignore the summons but in practice did so, and if any verdict was to be without effectiveness then the process would not resolve the dispute and certainly not so as to inhibit further unregulated conflict. But the attribute is not present in every legal system to the same extent. Again, where the 'court' has no power to issue a decision but only to make a recommendation that, it is conceded, the parties are not bound to follow, then the 'court' is not sufficiently authoritarian or authoritative to amount to a legal process.

The legal system of a modern state demonstrates the attribute at its fullest extent. If a private individual claims that another is in breach of contract and applies to the court of the state to resolve the dispute, not only will the court accept that it has jurisdiction, and, moreover, the supreme right of jurisdiction, but it will enforce its decision against an unwilling defendant. Of course, the courts of a state may have a hierarchical order, and appeal may be made from the decision of one court to a higher court. But until a decision is overturned by a higher court it is treated as correct. Within this structure the decision of the lower court is authoritative as far as outside bodies are concerned; only in that the decision may be overturned by an appeal court is it not authoritative.

The same applies to the making of legal rules. A law made by the territorial state's legislature is fully authoritative and authoritarian. Where the state grants power to make law to an individual or a body, the ensuing delegated legislation will also be authoritative and authoritarian but only in so far as it is within the powers granted to the individual or body.

But there has been a recent tendency for some territorial states to allow an action on certain grounds to be brought against them in the European Court of Human Rights by their own nationals. To the extent that a state has done so its own law has become less authoritative.

The attribute in question is, however, not so well marked in International law. States can only be brought before an international court if they so consent, and there is no effective organized system of sanctions. Normally there is no way of enforcing a decision of an international court and usually the best that can be hoped is that the state that loses the case will act in conformity with the judgement. Moreover, the state that loses may well deny the authority of the court or the decision, a claim that to some extent may be acquiesced in by the other party, who may try for some positive result through direct negotiation. It is these very features of International law (plus the absence of a legislature) that have led some scholars to deny the character of law to International law. Yet the attribute of being authoritarian and authoritative is by no means entirely absent from International law. In practice, states frequently do accept the jurisdiction of an International court and abide by its decision. In recent years, though, it must be admitted that the reputation of the World Court has suffered through the unwillingness of France and Iceland to have their disputes, with Australia and New Zealand in the one case and with Britain in the other, adjudicated by the court. States do give consent in general to proceedings before the World Court, although they may refuse consent in particular cases.

The law of a group (other than a state) will also possess the attribute, although usually to a very limited extent. Thus, if a minority church believes that one of its members has committed a serious offence against it, and it wishes to institute a trial, the individual may deny all right of jurisdiction to the church, pay no heed to the process, and ignore any sanction imposed on him. The supreme sanction available will in all probability be exclusion from membership of the church, and, should the individual no longer care about this, it is a very poor sanction indeed for serious wrongdoing. In fact, for some wrongs the church may want to call in the more authoritarian and authoritative law of the state. Of course, the group law may be much more authoritarian and authoritative than what has just been described. One need think only of the Holy Inquisition with its powers to seize suspected heretics and even infidels who had no connection whatever with Christianity, bring them before a regular court, torture them to extract evidence, and hand them over for execution if they were found guilty. An intermediate position might be held by the law of a professional organization. If (with the backing of the state) the organization has the power to prohibit a member from exercising his profession as, say, a doctor or lawyer, then its legal rules and process can be very authoritarian and authoritative. Such a sanction if it can be enforced ensures that in most cases the defendant will appear before the court and accept any lesser sanction that is imposed on him.

As with the rules of a group so with primitive law the extent to which this particular attribute is present can vary enormously from one people to another. Very frequently, no machinery will exist for the organized enforcement of a judgement. Even in a legal system as splendid and sophisticated as that of Rome of the Republic and early Empire, state machinery may be very largely lacking to compel a defendant to obey a summons to appear before a magistrate in respect of a private law suit—and without this appearance no action could proceed—or to enforce the judge's decision.[13]

This attribute of law of being authoritarian and authoritative is also therefore present in different systems to differing degrees. It is above all present in the law of a modern territorial state, and is little in evidence in International law. In group law and in primitive law its extent varies from group to group and from people to people.

(V)

Closely connected with the foregoing attribute is yet another typical feature of law and the legal process, the regulated sanction. By regulated sanction I mean that for failure to observe a legal rule the court imposes some sanction or punishment that is definite in extent (or reasonably so) and that will be enforced by persons appointed to that task. For instance, John makes a contract with William and fails to perform and is sued by William. If the court finds John is in breach of contract it will order him to pay a fixed sum by way of damages to William. If John fails to make payment, officers appointed by the court may seize his property, sell it and pay William out of the proceeds. This standard example can be contrasted with what happens when there is a breach of a moral obligation that is not also a legal obligation. There may well be a sanction—such as moral disapproval involving a break in cordial relations—but the extent of it will not be clearly defined, and the persons enforcing the sanction will not be appointed to that task.

Not every legal rule can really be said to be backed by a sanction, as John Austin claimed. Rules of evidence and of procedure must be accepted as rules of law, but no sanction can be found in them. Secondly, it is confusing to consider the nullity of a contract or of a testament, which is due to a failure to comply with the legal formalities, as a sanction; the rules merely withhold legal recognition from the contract or will.[14] And—to turn from the legal rules to the legal process—in some systems the court's decision is meant to reconcile the parties and not to impose punishment.

Yet, although not every legal rule and not every process involves a sanction, it is a characteristic feature of every type of legal system whether of a territorial state, International law, primitive law, of a group such as a trade union, that it operates with sanctions that are definite in extent. Within each type the characteristic may be more pronounced in one system than another. Thus, with respect to territorial states, the law of China is said traditionally to rely relatively little on sanctions.[15]

The other aspect of the regulated sanction, namely that it will be enforced by persons appointed to that task, does vary from one type of system to another but has already been treated in the preceding section, since it equally forms part of the attribute of law's being authoritative and authoritarian.

(VI)

A final typical attribute of law is that people regulate their behaviour by it, in other words law is obeyed. Thus for John Austin positive law is the command of a sovereign that is backed by a sanction, and the first characteristic of sovereignty that he lists is that 'The *bulk* of the given society are in a *habit* of obedience or submission'.[16] Even those who do not obey a law may regulate their conduct by it to an appreciable extent. Thus, a speed limit of 30 m.p.h. will persuade some drivers not to exceed 37 m.p.h. when otherwise they would have driven at 50 m.p.h.; or theftuously inclined persons may continue to steal but refrain from using violence.

But this attribute cannot be regarded as more typical of one type of legal system—that of territorial states for instance or International law—than of another. The degree of obedience obtained would depend on many other factors such as the apparent justice and fitness of the rule, and society's disapproval of any breach. Certain it is that International law is habitually obeyed.[17] States may be reluctant to accept the jurisdiction of the World Court, but they will go to very considerable lengths—notably, today, through holding international conferences—both to settle the law and to find out what it is. And when the law is known states will try to abide by it.

(VII)

In this chapter the nature of the typical attributes of law has been sketched. As was emphasised at the beginning, what appears as typical is to some extent dependent on one's standpoint. Hence it is reasonable, even if ethnocentric, for a Western jurist to emphasise as the basic typical attributes of law the very features that Western scholars have thought to be essential to law or to be the distinguishing marks of law.

But what has become plain is that the features that have been selected on the above basis as typical attributes of law exist in some types of legal systems more than in others. They are most apparent in the legal systems of territorial states, very much less so in International law. Depending on the particular body concerned, whether it be a trade union, professional organization or church, the individual typical attributes of law may be more or less in evidence in the group rules than they are in International law. The same applies to that large number of systems of varying degrees of complexity and sophistication which goes under the generic name of primitive law. Judged on the basis of these attributes some legal systems are more law-like than others, and the law of a modern territorial state is law *par excellence*.

In one sense that conclusion is inevitable, perhaps even banal, given the fact that the typical attributes were selected because they were considered fundamental by legal scholars who, in turn, regard state law as either the only law properly so called or at least the prime manifestation of law, with International law and primitive law ranking only as doubtful cases. But it should be remembered that it was these attributes, or some of them, which led scholars to the view that only state law was law; or was the prime manifestation of law. It is not the case that the starting point was the idea that only law of a territorial state is law, hence the attributes of state law were to be considered essential. This must be stressed, because it is vital to recognise that these typical attributes are in themselves extremely important for the notion of law in general.

It should also be emphasised that these typical attributes do not sharply separate the law of a territorial state from the legal rules of other groups; the distinction is one of degree rather than of kind.

Throughout the remainder of this book most attention will be paid to developed territorial law. This is partly because of the conclusion of this chapter that it is law *par excellence*, partly because all scholars, however restricted their idea of law may be, accept that in general it is law.

(VIII)

In the previous chapter it was maintained that some arbitration does not amount to a legal process, even though arbitration is the institutionalising of a dispute. When arbitration does not amount to a process the missing element is a decision.

Parties to a contract may insert a clause to the effect that in the event of a dispute an arbiter (selected in some specified way) will have power to give a binding ruling on the interpretation of the contract and the obligations of the parties. Should arbitration occur it will certainly be a legal process as envisaged here. There will be a dispute institutionalised with the specific object of inhibiting further unregulated conflict, and there will be a decision. It is reasonable to hold that the claims that give rise to it are claims of law, and that the decision is validated by law. The same is, of course, equally true of arbitration in terms of an Act of Parliament such as the Electricity Act 1947 or the Agricultural Holdings Act 1948, where the decision by the arbitral tribunal is binding and, in general, final.

But this does not hold true of some other forms of arbitration, for instance where there is a dispute between employer and employees over wage levels and the parties agree to have the matter heard before an arbiter whose recommendation, however, need not be accepted by the parties. The prime factor in declaring that this is not a legal process is that there is no decision saying 'this is the case' or 'you must do this'. The claim that initiates a legal process also demands a decision, not a recommendation. And, of course, since there is no decision in this case it cannot be claimed that law validates the decision.

The whole feeling of such arbitration is remote from that of a legal process. It is proper to emphasise that the arbitration here lacks an essential of the legal process, and thus that what is in issue is not primarily law, legal right or legal claim. But what is also striking (and has determined the position of this discussion) is the almost total absence in such arbitration of what I have called the typical attributes of law. The arbitration is not really part of a system; when it becomes regular it is in danger of being turned into a legal process. The arbitration is not usually set up by a person or body with the power to create law; usually the parties to the dispute jointly decide on the method of arbitration and the person of the arbiter. (It may be objected that it is at times a government that fixes the arbitration. But when this appears to happen, for example in Britain, the arbitration is not arranged by the sovereign in Parliament, which alone makes state law, but by declaration by the Prime Minister or by one or more of his Cabinet, who do not have power to make law.) The arbitral body does not act as if it was authoritative and authoritarian. Failure to observe the recommendation does not result in a regulated sanction imposed by the arbiters and enforced by persons appointed to that task. The recommendation, it must however be admitted, is likely to be obeyed, but only, it might be thought, if it is in accordance with the distribution of power among the protagonists and their allies.

Arbitration of this type should also be distinguished from a form of action that undoubtedly does involve a legal process, namely the action of declarator. This type of action, in Britain, is resorted to when no other remedy is available; for instance an action concluding for interdict or for specific performance—specific implement in Scotland—cannot be brought against the Crown. Such actions are brought before a court and the judgment is a declaration of the legal relationship between the parties and it is not accompanied by a sanction or any means of enforcing the judgment. But there is a proper judgment. And, as we have seen, the absence of a sanction or of means of enforcing a decision does not tell against the status of a legal process. In fact the authority of the court is great enough generally to restrain illegal conduct.[18]

There are other dispute situations institutionalised in a non-legal way where there is no danger of confusing the issues with legal rules or the debates with legal processes: for instance, the meeting of a church council to determine the attributes of a divinity. In this case the claim that initiated the council would be simply a claim of fact, not a claim of right. The decision will be validated only by the facts or supposed facts, not by the application to them of any rules that could remotely be considered to be legal rules. The essential function of the council will not be the inhibition of further unregulated conflict.

4

The Particular Virtues of Law

(I)

It seems to have emerged from the early chapters that law—taking legal rules and legal process together—has three essential functions. If the argument is correct then it would follow that any attribute of law that furthers any of the three essential functions has special importance. Thus any attribute that facilitates the resolution of a dispute by a process, or helps to validate the decision in the process or inhibit further unregulated conflict, has particular significance for the notion of law. The same would not, however, apply to an attribute that simply reduces the number of dispute situations since, as we have seen, it is not an essential function of law to restrict the number of dispute situations.[1]

It is an essential function of law to provide the means by which a dispute can be resolved in a process. But, as was argued earlier, it is not an essential of law to make a process inevitable in the event of a dispute. Indeed, some of the best legal rules, by their obvious equity and clarity, can obtain a good result without recourse to a process. Hence, it is not even necessarily a virtue of a legal rule that it makes a process inevitable or likely. But when that has been said it must also be claimed that it is a prime virtue of law to make a process readily available for the resolving of a dispute.

For law to make such a process readily available (1) the law must be known to be law, (2) the process must be within convenient reach of the persons affected, and (3) the legal rules must be easily knowable. This means that it is a particular virtue for law to be formally enacted and published, for its application to be within the financial and other means of the parties affected, and for the legal rules to be clear.

(II)

Formal enactment and publication may be considered together. Formal enactment means only that the legislation is passed in a way that makes plain that it is law and not something else, such as advice. Without the security of formal enactment behaviour may be treated as criminal on an apparently tyrannous whim. Formal enactment makes it easier both to have the dispute institutionalised and to have the decision in the process validated. Accordingly, territorial states, and many other groups as well, usually lay down expressly the steps required for the enactment of law. A failure to follow all the requisite steps prevents the legislation from being law.

Publication means that steps are taken to ensure that the precise contents of the law are accessible to all or at least to those directly affected by the law. Not surprisingly, many territorial states and other groups also require publication for a law's validity. But whereas formal enactment, except in an extreme tyranny, is treated as an integral part of legislation, publication need not be regarded as part of the law-making process. A failure in formal enactment will mean that no law comes into existence; a failure in publication may have that result but may equally entail that the law, which has been validly created, cannot be enforced.[2]

But in practice, even in a representative democracy, the government or a Minister or officials will at times determine that a legal rule should not be published. Other factors, such as national security, are thought in some circumstances to have greater importance than has a prime virtue of law. For example, after World War Two, the National Service Acts in Britain gave the Minister of Labour and National Service power to exempt by regulation categories of persons from compulsory military service. Although these regulations were issued to civil servants in Ministry of Labour offices they were treated as confidential, and their precise contents were not made available to the general public.

(III)

By the same token it is a particular virtue of law that the process be within ready reach of the persons involved in a dispute. If not, the process cannot easily be used, the dispute will not be regulated, recourse will not be had to the law—or when it is, only at great suffering and inconvenience—and a dangerous feeling of injustice may arise.

In the first instance, ready reach must mean ready financial reach. In other words, the cost of litigation ought to be such that a person with a reasonable legal claim (or defence) need not feel deterred on that account from proceeding with his claim or defence. Still more it means that a person who proceeds with such a claim or defence and is unsuccessful should not find that the legal costs seriously affect his style of life, because the result would be to discourage others from allowing law to regulate disputes. Unfortunately this particular virtue is lacking in many contemporary countries, where the cost of litigation may be enormous and out of proportion to the means of the parties. The situation seems to be particularly objectionable when the financial suffering falls unevenly because one party is wealthy or entitled to legal aid and can use this advantage to deter the other from pursuing or defending to the proper extent.

Various means of combating the present defect might be suggested—for instance, nationalization of legal services, forms of insurance—but they are not relevant to the present study. What should be stressed, however, is that if the general argument of this book is correct then it is more proper, and a better fulfilment of its service to society, that law should ensure that disputes can in practice be institutionalised rather than devise the best possible legal rule for that particular society; and, *a fortiori*, that the law should ensure this is preferable to having the court interpret the law correctly (since, as we shall see, it is not always the case that the law in force is actually the best that can be devised). All these ends, of course, are desirable and they may not be mutually exclusive. But should financial stringencies impose the choice, the balance should be decisively tipped towards the institutionalising of disputes. There should be ready access to the courts for all, even if as a financial consequence the courts had to be staffed by judges of lower intellectual rating, the chain of appeals to successive higher courts diminished and a strict limit imposed on the number of days allowed for a court hearing. In such circumstances, the quality of the legal rules (and therefore, at least to some extent, of the individual decisions) could be maintained—especially in the Common Law world—by increasing the weight given to academic legal opinion. A system of precedent is not a cheap way of building up legal rules.

It should be observed that the conclusions—first, that access to the courts should be readily available to all without imposing financial hardship, and secondly, that, where circumstances made a choice inevitable, the institutionalising of dispute situations should be preferred to having the highest possible standards of judging individual cases—have been reached not on the basis of what may be claimed to be justice but through a consideration of the prime virtues of law that derive directly from the essential functions of law.

Again, if access to the process is to be readily available then, apart even from financial considerations, legal advice ought to be easily obtained by means of, for instance, neighbourhood law centres. This conclusion, too, derives from the same notion of law.

(IV)

Thirdly, law will not make a process readily available to resolve a dispute unless the law is reasonably clear. Normally a process cannot be initiated unless a prospective plaintiff has reason to believe that he has a case at law, and for this he must, within narrow limits, know what the law is. Of course it will happen in any system that there will be doubt as to the precise meaning and scope of some rules of law, and also that there will be situations in which, though the facts may not be in dispute, the case involves naturally tricky questions of law. Borderline cases are inevitable. But what is at issue here is that existing legal rules should be so expressed that they are fairly readily comprehensible to the persons affected. Such a claim may influence our view as to the best system of law that can be envisaged in practice.

In general, a system of law established primarily by custom or case law will set out the legal rules less clearly than a system based predominantly on statute, and the latter system in its turn must yield primacy in clarity to a system based on a code. Of course, it is possible to imagine a code so badly drafted or administered that it is incomprehensible in its working, but it seems safe to state that the best conceivable code will be clearer than the best conceivable series of statutes, which in turn will present the law in a clearer way than the best system of precedent.

It has, of course, often been observed that codes and statutes do not give a clear legal answer in all situations—neither does precedent—and this may cast doubt on their clarity or on the importance of clarity. A very instructive passage occurs in Eugen Ehrlich:[3]

> Everyone who has compared a statute with a book that has been written about it has observed that the bulk of the book is many times greater than that of the statute, occasionally as much as several hundred times greater. The idea suggests itself to inquire into the cause of this phenomenon. How did it come about that so large a volume was written about so brief a statute? To this question the jurists have a very plausible answer at hand. Every statute, be it never so clear and detailed, leaves room for all manner of doubt. To resolve these doubts is the function of juristic literature. Now the doubts must be rather great if they can be resolved only in books that are of so much greater size than the statutes themselves. Under these circumstances, I take it, the further question is justified: Why are the statutes not couched in terms that leave no room for doubt? For nothing is gained under our present-day method if, in order to arrive at a clear understanding of what the statute ordains, one must refer to a book that has been written about it. The statutes therefore ought to be more detailed or juristic literature is superfluous.

His own explanation of the difference follows:

> Further inquiry will convince one that the difference between a statute and a book that discusses the statute is not quantitative but qualitative. The juristic books do not offer something additional but something different. For they contain the juristic technique, practical juristic science. Technique is out of place in a statute.

Ehrlich's observation is, of course, acute, but I suggest that the 'very plausible answer' of the jurists is much more to the point, especially if it is given greater particularity. In the first place the authors of the books in question do not have authority to make law in the same way as have the legislators. They persuade by means of the quality of their reasoning, not by any formal position they hold. Hence, in the commentaries much space is taken up by a discussion of the nature of the legal problem, by setting out the various possible answers, and by justifying the solution proposed and preferred by the authors. The statute, on the other hand, only has to state the rule.

Secondly, and more significantly, the commonly remarked shortness of a statute compared with a commentary on it is primarily to be attributed to a combination of difference in audience and in function. In general the statute is addressed to the public at large; the commentary to legal experts or those who would become such. In general the function of the statute is to regulate the typical so that guide lines are provided for future conduct; the function of the commentary is to explain the marginal to the expert, and to place the legislation in its context.

In these circumstances it is not surprising that the commentary is normally longer than the statute. The statute should be couched in general terms whereas the commentary should concentrate on particular acts or facts in detailed circumstances. Complicated individual situations must be discussed in the latter. Simplicity is a great virtue in statute, and with simplicity, where possible, brevity, even though, as Plato rightly claimed, 'It is high quality that we should value, I think, not extreme brevity or length'.[4] No one would dispute the great importance of having substantive law of high quality, and we need not discuss that issue at the moment.

Consequently, it will not be a serious reproach to the legal draftsman that the statute does not provide for every eventuality that can be imagined or that does in fact arise. Indeed, if the statute did so provide it would be so bulky as to be inaccessible. But it will be cause for blame if the statute does not deal with the typical situations fully enough for the ordinary person to know in some detail what his legal rights are. And it will be a fault in a legal system that commentaries of weight do not become available. The point that a statute does not and need not provide for every eventuality is obvious, yet failure to appreciate it lies at the root of the commonest criticisms of codification in the English-speaking world, namely that a code does not remove the need for interpretation, that doubts remain and further law is built up on the basis of the code, and that the law is not entirely clear to the layman.[5]

It has recently been claimed that the importance of the intelligibility of law is distinctly overrated and that 'the reality is that no matter how laws are drafted, the vast majority of the populace have only the vaguest notion of the vast majority of them'.[6] The statement is true enough, but we should remember that for the vast majority of the populace the vast majority of laws have no direct relevance for their conduct or for the exercise of their rights. They do not need to know the legal rules. The same author pointed out that sociological investigation had shown that the Norwegian Housemaid Law of 1948 was not understood by housewives or housemaids and that its mere existence (probably with other factors such as increasing scarcity of domestic labour) produced much of the desired effect. This argument, I believe, is rather beside the point. Except when he has an actual dispute, which can be settled by law, the lay person's knowledge of a law will be derived from secondary sources such as newspapers and television. In these circumstances it is important that the reporters can understand the law and transmit the gist of it. When a dispute actually arises, it is important that the lay person can and does understand the law and know his rights, and likewise here the law's clarity is of great importance.

It has also been pointed out that at times legal forms are deliberately couched in misleading terms.[7] This practice, can, of course, be highly advantageous to those responsible for the drafting but tells us nothing about the general significance of clarity in law.

(V)

Within the framework of the process it is an essential function of law to validate the decision. Hence, anything that helps with this validation is also a particular virtue of law.

From this it follows first of all that it is a particular virtue that reasons be given for the legal decision. If no explanation is available of how the court reached its conclusion, it will not be easy to see how legal rules interacted with the facts, or apparent facts, to give the verdict. There are two aspects of this. First, the grounds of decision should be made known to the parties; secondly, to the public at large. On occasion plausible arguments, for instance national security, might be adduced for the wisdom of not publishing to the public at large the facts of a particular case—and, if the facts are not given, how the law was applied to them will also not be clear—but no really convincing argument exists for not disclosing to the parties the grounds of the legal decision. It will be apparent that this virtue of law not only helps to validate the decision but also to inhibit further unregulated conflict. When one knows how the law is interpreted and enforced one can regulate one's conduct accordingly.

In practice, where the grounds of a decision are not given the explanation is usually nothing more than administrative convenience, since, if the reasons for a decision are not given, the decision cannot be attacked for faulty or unpersuasive argumentation. In very special circumstances this itself might be seen as a particular virtue. Thus it is related that a General, who had been appointed governor of an island in the West Indies, was in perplexity at having to decide cases when he had never previously been in court. Lord Mansfield gave him advice:

> Be of good cheer—take my advice, and you will be reckoned a great judge as well as a great commander-in-chief. Nothing is more easy; only hear both sides patiently—then consider what you think justice requires, and decide accordingly. But never give your reasons;—for your judgment will probably be right, but your reasons will certainly be wrong.

When the General first forgot the advice and gave reasons, their ludicrous absurdity resulted in an appeal in which he was suspected of corruption.[8]

Juries do not give reasons for their verdict, but that fact is not really in point in this section. In a jury trial it is the function of the judge to explain to the jury (and hence to the populace at large) what the legal rules are, and the jury finds on the facts and applies the law to them. Thus, the judge's summing-up amounts to a statement of the legal reasons for the eventual decision.

Similarly, established procedures should be observed in the process. For instance, to allow evidence of a kind not allowed before, or change the onus of proof, or permit a judge suddenly to take a more active rôle than previously in examining the parties and witnesses, will positively militate against any decision being acceptable.

More particularly with regard to inhibiting further unregulated conflict, it is likewise a particular legal virtue that there should be a high level of consistency in legal judgements. Similar cases should be decided alike. Such a practice is also needed so that one can regulate one's behaviour to avoid future conflict. Nothing in this statement, of course, should be taken as meaning that there ought to be a binding system of precedent.

(VI)

Some of what I have called the particular virtues of law are considered by others to be part of natural law or justice. Indeed, Lon Fuller[9] regards two of them, namely publication to the affected party and clarity, as being among the eight elements of what he regards as 'the morality which makes law possible'. The total failure of any of these elements would, in his view, result in something that could not be regarded as a legal system at all. It should, however, be emphasised that in the present book the high value attributed to the 'particular virtues' derives from the concept of the essential functions of law and not from any arguments as to morality or justice. But some features to be found in law and in the process, which are usually valued highly, do not appear, and cannot appear, on the list of particular virtues of law. Among these, pride of place must be given to the propositions that past behaviour should not retrospectively be made criminal, and that the parties to a law suit should be treated alike. The reason these features do not appear is that, if the present analysis is correct, their value derives from the moral perspectives of society and not from law's essential functions.

A law that makes past behaviour criminal need not be in opposition in any way to the essential functions of law. Past behaviour is only likely to be made criminal when it is regarded as so offensive as to cause serious disputes: the law can institutionalise these and validate the decision. Moreover, the process will have the specific object of inhibiting further unregulated conflict in respect of that which gave rise initially to the law and will also restrain future conduct of the kind now treated as criminal.

Similarly, in a society where very marked differences of status are socially accepted, differences in the application of the law to persons of different status need not detract from the essential functions of law and the legal process. Indeed, for a court to fail to mark these differences in treatment might give rise to unregulated conflict.

5

The Force that Backs Law

(I)

In a fundamental sense, law is about 'order'. Law's essential functions are to institutionalise disputes, validate the decisions given in the process and inhibit unregulated conflict. All three functions relate to 'order'. But law cannot perform these functions or any of its other functions unless it has an authority that is recognised. This authority is made up of two elements: force or violence to back up the law, and respect for the law. In this chapter we will discuss the former alone.

But first let me give a quotation from Xenophon, not because it states a self-evident truth but because it is illuminating for attitudes.

> Indeed, there is a story told of Alcibiades, that, when he was less than twenty years old, he had a talk about laws with Pericles, his guardian, the first citizen in the State.
>
> 'Tell me, Pericles,' he said, 'can you teach me what a law is?'
>
> 'Certainly,' he replied.
>
> 'Then pray teach me. For whenever I hear men praised for keeping the laws, it occurs to me that no one can really deserve that praise who does not know what a law is.'
>
> 'Well, Alcibiades, there is no great difficulty about what you desire. You wish to know what a law is. Laws are all the rules approved and enacted by the majority in assembly, whereby they declare what ought and what ought not to be done.'
>
> 'Do they suppose it is right to do good or evil?'
>
> 'Good, of course, young man,—not evil.'
>
> 'But if, as happens under an oligarchy, not the majority, but a minority meet and enact rules of conduct, what are these?'

'Whatsoever the sovereign power in the State, after deliberation, enacts and directs to be done is known as a law.'

'If, then, a despot, being the sovereign power, enacts what the citizens are to do, are his orders also a law?'

'Yes, whatever a despot as ruler enacts is also known as a law.'

'But force, the negation of law, what is that, Pericles? Is it not the action of the stronger when he constrains the weaker to do whatever he chooses, not by persuasion, but by force?'

'That is my opinion.'

'Then whatever a despot by enactment constrains the citizens to do without permission, is the negation of law?'

'I think so: and I withdraw my answer that whatever a despot enacts without persuasion is a law.'

'And when the minority passes enactments, not by persuading the majority, but through using its power, are we to call that force or not?'

'Everything, I think, that men constrain others to do "without persuasion", whether by enactment or not, is not law, but force.'

'It follows then, that whatever the assembled majority, through using its power over the owners of property, enacts without persuasion is not law, but force?'

'Alcibiades,' said Pericles, 'at your age, I may tell you, we, too, were very clever at this sort of thing. For the puzzles we though about and exercised our wits on were just such as you seem to think about now.'

'Ah, Pericles,' cried Alcibiades, 'if only I had known you intimately when you were at your cleverest in these things!'[1]

(II)

From our minimum definition of law it emerged that law institutionalises disputes by a process that has the specific object of inhibiting further unregulated conflict. It might therefore appear to the unwary—as it did to Alcibiades in the passage from Xenophon quoted in the preceding section—that law and force (or violence) are irreconcilable enemies. This is far from being the truth. A great part—some might say all—of law's effectiveness derives from the fact that legal decisions can be enforced. For some scholars, rules that cannot be enforced cannot be law. Thus on the one hand, law exists above all for the sake of order. On the other, law relies for its existence on its support from violence; or at least, law to be effective is usually provided with support from violence. And, to complicate the issue further, it is the law (or the law makers) that decides what violence is to be regarded as permissible and what is not. There is, however, here no confusion, no paradox, and no arbitrariness. It is the force which can control the force of others or is the strongest force among those in conflict that determines both what is law and what the law is, and hence decides what violence is to be outside the law and what inside. This has to be so, since otherwise the appropriate process could not have the specific object of inhibiting unregulated conflict. We should add that 'the force which can control the force of others or is the strongest force among those in conflict' may well have moral authority as part of its strength. One example will suffice for the moment.

Let us imagine an established government that is faced with an internal guerilla group, which it has difficulty in crushing and which is supported by a minority of the populace but actively opposed by the majority. The guerillas hold no recognizable territory and, so far as can be foreseen, have no realistic prospect of taking power from the government. Both the government troops and the guerillas seize some of each other's men, subject them to a process based on rules and, after a verdict of guilty, execute them. Violence has been carried out on both sides under a claim of legality. Naturally, each side condemns the other's behaviour as unlawful. The process conducted by the guerillas can in no way be considered a legal process since in no meaningful sense can one objectively claim that its object is to inhibit further unregulated conflict. Nor, subjectively, would the guerillas or outsiders believe that the specific object of the process was to inhibit further unregulated conflict. The process conducted by the government, on the other hand, can be considered a legal process. Its object will be to inhibit further unregulated conflict. It may or may not have that effect in practice, but many will believe that it has, or at least that the process should occur with that purpose in view. Therefore, not only would the trial be a legal process, but the rules that call it into existence and that validate the decision will be legal rules.

The strength of the established government—and also to some extent its moral authority—will be shown by the fact that it conducts processes that can be considered legal processes on many other matters, especially civil matters, which have nothing whatever to do with the conflict with the guerillas. The guerillas' processes will in the main be involved with this conflict and will be limited in range, above all to matters treated as criminal.

(III)

The main concern of this chapter, however, the rôle of force that backs law, is best approached in two parts: first, whether law can ever need the backing of so much force that it forfeits the name of law; secondly, whether there can ever be law that has no backing of force.

Let us start from common ground. No legal philosopher would, I think, seriously dispute that the legislature of a representative democracy such as the United Kingdom passes statutes that count as real law. Yet this law is backed by force. If a man commits murder (and is caught) he will be arrested, tried and punished. If he commits a breach of contract, the other party to the contract may sue him, and the award of damages made by the court will be enforced by the state against him, however unwilling he might be to accede to the court's order. Although force may not be an essential of law, it is clear that it can be an integral part. At the very least, law does not cease to be law because it is backed by force. (The question whether law would cease to be law if it was not backed by force is to be left till later.) But the example raises questions of the acceptance of the law, consent to the law, and approval of the law.

Clearly the law, to be law, does not need the unforced acceptance, consent and approval of everyone, including those against whom it is enforced. But does it of the majority? If for the moment one reduces discussion to the question whether a statute, say, is law only if the majority prefers to have it than not to have it, then the answer is no. The preference of the majority does not affect the status of the statute as law. For example, in a system such as that of the U.K. it is perfectly possible for one political party, say Labour, to win a majority of seats in Parliament even though more votes are cast for its nearest rival, the

Conservative party, and although other parties also receive a sizable proportion of the votes. If a Labour government, to keep the support of its own left-wing members, had a statute passed that was unpopular with some other labour voters, the U.K. could have a law that a very sizable majority of the populace would prefer not to have.[2] Yet the status of the statute as law is beyond dispute. One cannot say that the majority of the populace has unforcedly accepted, or consented to, or approved of, this particular law. One might, however, say that they have acquiesced in the law. Or perhaps it might be argued that they have consented to a legal system of which this statute forms part.

The latter alternative can be ruled out. Consent to the whole (legal system) does not necessarily entail consent to, or acquiescence in, the part (the statute). Violent opposition to a particular statute may arise without any desire to overthrow the system or government by force. As a consequence of such opposition the bill may be withdrawn before it becomes law, or the law may be set aside by the legislators, and the legal system or government may be left intact. Here there could be consent to the whole but no acquiescence in the part. Moreover, consent to the whole, as distinct from acquiescence in the whole, does not seem relevant at all in this connection. Imagine law made by the English Parliament at a date when only a minority had any right to vote. Are we to say that the whole system of statutes is not law because the majority has not consented? Surely not. The absurdity of any other answer is shown if we consider the consequences of an extension of the franchise. Let us imagine that universal suffrage is granted and that no drastic legislation to change the legal system is introduced. The old statutes will be regarded as fully in force and must surely be now considered by us to be valid. Yet if they were not law before, what makes them law now? Consent—which would have to mean tacit consent—cannot be the answer. Any argument that it was would of necessity be so obviously artificial as to need no refutation. Thus, rules that appear to be legal rules passed by an unrepresentative government and that are acquiesced in by the populace are true legal rules.

Thus, for law to be law, acquiescence—which may be unwilling—is the very most that may be required, certainly not consent to it or approval of it. But what if there is not acquiescence, but open rebellion? Then we are back in the situation described in the second section of this chapter. Provided the government retains control of the strongest force, then even if the majority of the populace support the rebellion, the government's processes will be proper legal processes, and its apparent legal rules will be real law. But violent rebellion is not a stable condition; a situation at rest without unlawful violence will be sought; and the force that emerges as the strongest, whether the existing government, a new government of different type or a compromise,[3] will want acquiescence in its legal rules.

Thus, force backs law to secure acquiescence in the law.[4] Since this is the function of force in this context, and since it is specifically the force which controls other force that determines what is law it cannot be claimed that law which is ultimately acquiesced in is ever backed by so much force as to cease to be law.

(IV)

But the preceding section raises the question whether law remains law if during a rebellion the sitting of the courts has to be temporarily suspended. Or if a new law is passed, which because of the troubled conditions never gives rise to a process before a court, is this law? Or, in peaceable circumstances, if a statute is never used in a country whose legal system does not recognise any doctrine of desuetude, does it remain law?

The last question may be answered first since it presents no real problem. The statute continues to be law. It still remains the means adopted to institutionalise dispute situations and to validate decisions given in the appropriate process, and so on. It can still be used when necessary. The only thing lacking is a dispute, and should such arise the law could be invoked to call the process into being. There is nothing in the notion of law which demands that an appropriate dispute arise at least once each month, or each year or each century.

When the sitting of courts is suspended because of rebellion the law will remain law. The reasons for this assertion are, first, that until the government is actually overthrown the assumption will be that the sittings are only temporarily suspended and processes will eventually resume on the basis of the existing law;

and, secondly, the further assumption that any incoming régime will in effect treat the old law as law. The probability is that on many matters the new rulers will simply accept the old law as continuing law; even where they do not, they will usually declare the old rules abrogated, thus giving them the status of law up until that moment.

A third factor must be stressed here, which has the greatest psychological impact. Rules and statutes, even very new ones, which give rise to no processes, will be regarded as law because they are the work of, or are upheld by a government that has been recognised, however unwillingly, to have law-creating powers. Until that government is toppled, its recent enactments —cast in the same form as its enactments that undoubtedly were law—will be thought of as being law.

Thus, in a time of rebellion, when the courts are suspended, the law remains law. It is not even necessarily ineffective since juristic acts, such as marriages or contracts, concluded in this period may well subsequently be given their effect in accordance with the law that existed at this time.

It may be worth observing that such a period of rebellion presents at least as many apparent difficulties for the Austinian Positivists' view of law as it does for us. For them law is a command of a sovereign that is backed by a sanction, and by definition the command of a sovereign is habitually obeyed. But during the rebellion and before the government is actually overthrown, the law promulgated by the government, the supposed sovereign, may not be habitually obeyed. And during the suspension of the courts the sovereign's command may lack a sanction.

(V)

Can law exist without force or violence to support it? The answer should be sought above all in International law, which, be it noted, is also lacking in some of the typical attributes of law that make the law of a national state law *par excellence*. Any answer to our question will provoke opposition, partly because some legal philosophers would deny the title of law to International law, partly because different nations, or groups of nations, view International law in different ways. There is among International lawyers of different countries no fundamental agreement as to the character of International law, and dispute even rages as to the possibility of general International law existing between states of different ideology.[6]

Still, we must proceed as best as we can. On the argument put forward in this book, International law is real law since it institutionalises disputes in a process that has the specific object of inhibiting further unregulated conflict.

The question of force or violence backing International law is best approached in two stages: disputes affecting territorial integrity, then more minor disputes.

In the past the international legal system as a whole claimed that territorial integrity rested upon the acquiescence of states. This amounted to saying that the possession of territory by a 'sovereign' prince or state was something that the legal system did not have the power or authority to change. States, therefore, were provided with a measure of guarantee of their territorial integrity even though their possession of territory or the legitimacy of their possession rested on conquest, enforced peace treaties, or immemorial possession.

Yet there was possibly a threadbare quality in this legal order that led many to the view—which, however, was never dominant—that acquiescence was a notional or fictional concept that jurists had projected onto a system of relations in which force dominated to such an extent that there was no point in speaking of law as playing a part. It was accepted by all that conquest and enforced peace treaties constituted valid titles to territory—after all, they were responsible for the boundaries and existence of most states—and this, coupled with the legal doctrine that permitted states a virtually unlimited right to go to war, gave force, it was felt, an important rôle in International law. Certainly it was widely, though not universally, accepted that this right of going to war should be exercised only in defence of existing legal rights;[7] but since there was no independent authority to determine whether a war supposedly waged in defence of existing rights was justified, a virtually unrestricted right to wage war was allowed.

On this basis one could say that International law (relating to territorial integrity) formerly consisted of a Law of Peace which rested on acquiescence, but this Law of Peace could at any time be replaced by the Law of War. Wars, however, would end; the

Law of Peace would again come to apply. The standard situation involved, therefore, the Law of Peace, which was not backed by force or violence.

That was formerly the position. It is now very difficult to define the place of acquiescence in the present international legal system. War has been outlawed! Lawyers, with very few exceptions, write textbooks only on the Law of Peace. Nonetheless, it does seem to be generally admitted that in a legal system that has no institutions to facilitate change, a Law of Peace on its own involves placing too high a weight on the possibility of acquiescence in the existing order. Ideology[8] or principle, especially the principle of self-determination of peoples, means that there is a general unwillingness to accept every situation of fact as having the traditional legal consequences; for instance, the legal status of Israel, Rhodesia and Formosa is in all cases disputed, although in the nineteenth century all three would, without difficulty, have been recognised as states. This controversy is clearly illustrated in the difficulty experienced in defining aggression within the United Nation's context. Yet it is precisely here that in the view of some law is backed by violence. Thus, the principle of self-determination of peoples, when joined with the argument that force is justified to secure self-determination, amounts to the claim that the law or legal right is backed by (lawful) force or violence. Again, the Brezhnev doctrine, at least as understood by the Soviet Union, is to the effect that 'Socialist brotherhood' permits intervention by force in the internal affairs of a socialist country by other such countries. On this basis the Soviet Union publicly defended its invasion of Czechoslovakia in August 1968. On this view of the law, too, a legal right in International law is backed by force.

All in all, it seems that International law relating to territorial integrity is a system of law that is not backed by force or violence; but there are exceptions or purported exceptions.[9]

The second stage of the discussion concerns the place of force in resolving minor disputes among states. The position this time is not so controversial. Force or violence does not back International law as it does the law of a state. Power, of course, is dispersed among the individual nations, hence in general there is no possibility of compelling complete conformity by a state to a legal rule. Authority is also dispersed and there is no independent body able to declare both that state A has violated the law and that states B and C have the legal right of imposing sanctions by force.

Instead, there is general acceptance of particular consequences of the principle of the sovereign equality of states. Law is almost always a product of agreement among states. This agreement, which is expressed in treaties, rests upon reciprocity. So if one state neglects its side of the bargain the other is entitled to readjust the balance accordingly. For instance, if both states agree to lower import controls and one goes back on its promise the other state is entitled to react to the same extent. There is a sanction here, but it cannot be said that the law is backed by force or violence in the sense in which I have been using the terms in this chapter. In many cases, too, even an economic sanction of this sort cannot be used, either because the injured state has already performed its side of the bargain or because the imposition of such a sanction could hurt it more.[10] In many cases the real sanction that would result from a state's breaking a treaty is the loss of esteem or trust of other states. Since the number of states is small, breaches of International law by one state can easily be known to all others.

It would, therefore, seem to be the case that International law relating to minor disputes among nations is law that is not backed by force or violence.[11]

All in all, therefore, International law appears to have little backing from violence or force. In some situations, with regard to territorial integrity, theory allows that legal rights can be enforced by violence.[12] Yet, at the very least, we can say that if a legal system depended for its existence on the support it could receive from lawful violence then International law as a system would not exist. More than that, International law enables us to envisage, at least in theory, a system of law not at all backed by violence, whose existence rests on acquiescence and respect coupled with non-violent sanctions. International law proves—though I believe no proof was necessary—that the reasons for observing law are not restricted to the force or violence that the system may call into play.

The law of a nation state unbacked by force or violence is, on the other hand, inconceivable. This is not to say, of course, that in such a system every rule must be supported by a sanction.

Nor does it mean that the force or violence has to be directly supplied by the state. As has been mentioned before, in Rome of the Republic and early Empire the state did little, if anything, to compel the defendant in a private action to appear—and without appearance the action could not proceed—or, if he lost the action, to enforce the judgment. But self-help by the plaintiff was lawful; that violence backed the law, and account of it was taken by the legal system.

But in respect of what might be called low-level law, we can now imagine a system unbacked by violence. Thus, a church makes legal rules governing the conduct of its members, and the members on the whole follow these rules out of respect. A dispute, however, occurs and gives rise to a process, which the defendant loses. He is ordered by the court to perform some act by way of amends. The church may lack machinery for enforcing the judgment, but the defendant may, however reluctantly, feel obliged to perform, either because of the (moral ?) authority of the church, or out of respect for the law, or to keep the good opinion of his fellow-members. Should the defendant fail to perform the church may have no further sanction at its disposal, or it may threaten and even enforce exclusion from its membership. In either eventuality there would be a legal system that is not backed by violence. Should the defendant refuse to accept his exclusion and, say, causes a breach of the peace, he may be restrained and punished by the law of the state, which is backed by force. It could be said that the law of the church has behind it the law of the state. But at least in some cases the better analysis would be that the church law was a separate system, and the state was intervening not to support the church court's ruling but to punish a breach of the peace.

(VI)

Finally, as an appendix it is appropriate to add a little to the discussion in this chapter and in chapter 2 of guerilla groups and law. I declared that at times the rules and processes of guerilla groups amount to law and at other times they do not.

Let us now imagine an urban guerilla group operating in a district where it has at least the tacit support of a proportion of the inhabitants, and where it has considerable authority over the population, even though in a full-scale battle with the forces of the state it would lose, and even though it shares its authority over the population with the state. The guerillas may use institutionalised processes to resolve disputes, even in non-criminal matters, between persons in the population who, however, are not members of the guerilla group. Such processes and the relevant rules that are brought into issue may, or may not, be legal. Everything depends on the actual factual relationship, especially between the process and rules of the guerilla group, on the one hand, and those of the state on the other. If the population acquiesce in the processes, and especially if defeated parties do not call the state in aid, and if the forces of the state do not actively seek to overturn the practical effects of the processes, then (if other conditions are satisfied) the processes—especially if there is a regular pattern to them—can properly be regarded as legal processes and the rules in them as law. Persons who are not members of the guerilla group may be very happy to accept the authority of the guerilla process. The judgment may be much cheaper, far less remote and every bit as just as that of the state court, and may resolve the dispute equally well. In my view it is reasonable to accept that the Dáil Courts, which were set up by Sinn Féin in 1919 to administer law distinct from that of the British government courts in Ireland, and which from the government viewpoint were not lawful courts, were real legal processes dealing with real law. In general, their authority was accepted and they did resolve disputes and inhibit further unregulated conflict.[13]

It is even easier to concede that the hearing is a fully legal one when the parties to the dispute are members of the guerilla group—indeed this is true in general of hearings held under the rules of a group. The reason is that the parties are then still more inclined to accept the authority of the 'court', the state is less likely to intervene, and hence it is less difficult for the essential function of a legal process to be satisfied.

6

Legal Rules and Society

(I)

It might be suggested that this book presents a misleading picture of the nature of law since chapter 1 constrains the reader to work within my terms of reference, which do not extend to the relationship between law on the one hand and the ethics, metaphysics and power structure of a given society on the other. Certainly, in the early chapters of this book the legal process appeared more prominently than did legal rules; and, indeed, legal rules were considered primarily in relation to their function in the legal process. Yet when a legal rule affects social life it usually does so—I would concede—without actually involving a process. It will be remembered that in my view, although the essential and distinguishing feature of law and the legal rule is the process, the central feature of law is the possibility or the threat of a process. To understand the nature of law and its rôle in society we must consider not only the theoretical aspect of its essential functions but also the practical relationship between legal rules and the society in which they operate, and the factors that determine how legal rules develop.

Law, I have been arguing, exists essentially for the sake of order, and hence law and legal rules act as a control upon human behaviour. But it is well known that very many legal rules go beyond mere controlling and actually direct human behaviour along specified channels. As was mentioned at an earlier point, the channelling function is often the most prominent, and the essential function is concealed in the background. No precise distinction can be drawn between 'controlling' and 'channelling', but the difference is nevertheless clear. For instance, a law may declare that contracts can be proved only in particular ways. But the state is not directing people to make contracts nor is there really any strong desire on the part of the state that individuals should make contracts according to particular formalities. The desire is rather that disputes as to whether or not a contract was in fact made should be avoided or easily resolved. Generally speaking, any formalities which would achieve that aim would have been acceptable to the state. Such a law would be an example of controlling. On the other hand a law that required all young men to serve in the army for two years, when there was no obvious emergency, would be channelling.

Often there are several possible rules that could be enacted; the choice of any one will satisfy the requirement of order, although the choice actually made will have effects upon the society. Nonetheless, if my claim is correct that law is essentially about order and that law has no essential function independent of order or in addition to order, then we should expect—contrary to the view of other theorists who have considered the matter—that there need not be anything like an exact correlation between the political, social and economic needs and desires of the members of a society as a whole or of its ruling élite on the one hand and the legal rules actually existing in the society on the other. On this view of law, society should be able and willing to tolerate legal rules that are not—and are known to be not—the most efficient that could be devised. It must be emphasised that the real choice of rule is restricted to those rules that will not bring about disorder (though on occasion mistakes will be made). The function to channel behaviour is not itself an essential function of a legal rule—although in any developed legal system some or many rules will channel behaviour—and is always, I believe, subordinate to law's essential functions in respect of order.[1]

(II)

It must be admitted that theorists who have written in the past do consider that an intimate relationship exists between legal rules and the society in which they operate.[2] A general statement to that effect is to be found in Montesquieu,[3] who claimed that laws are so particular to the people for whom they are made that 'it is the merest chance if those of one nation can suit another'. Later writers have tried to particularise this relationship.

The famous Friedrich von Savigny claimed[4] that positive law lived in the common consciousness of the people, that law was not produced from the arbitrary will of individuals, but was created by the spirit of the people (Volksgeist) that was in all the individuals together. This rather mystical conception has been much criticised—how is one to define a people, or explain Germany's dependence on Roman law at the time Savigny was writing, or account for the minutest legal technicalities ?—but it still retains a vigorous life in the writings of contemporary scholars.[5] Moreover, Savigny, whose practical aim was to prevent the promulgation of a Civil Code for Germany, was successful in delaying the Code for half a century.[6]

Harvard's Dean Roscoe Pound in his turn, following upon Rudolf von Ihering, maintained that law was social engineering.[7] Whatever theories of law were in favour, he argued, the legal order from Roman times onwards was in actual fact securing as much as possible of the scheme of interests with the least friction and waste, and this it was doing remarkably well.

For the Marxists, law is simply the expression of other relations upon which state power rests. The material life of individuals, which is independent of their 'will', is the real basis of the state (that is, of a state in which division of labour and private property are necessary). These relations are not created by state power; in fact, it is they that create state power. The people who rule in such circumstances make law, which is determined by these relations and which is independent of their idealistic will.[8] Neither Karl Marx nor Friedrich Engels attempted to develop a full theory of law: for them, law was one aspect of the state; but the fundamental view of their followers may be summed up as 'All law is class law'.[9]

Yet another view—which this time is restricted to primitive law—insists that there exists a general pattern of development that is common to early systems.[10]

All these theories are united in the basic tenet that law stands in a close rational or *the* natural (inevitable) relationship with society, to the needs or desires of the people or its ruling élite. Most of them, however, also postulate or allow for some divergence of law from these needs or desires. Thus it was fundamental to Savigny's practical case that statutory law and, even more, a code could be in breach of the Volksgeist.[11] Among Marxists, Engels claimed that law seeks an internally coherent expression and thus fails to be a faithful reflection of economic conditions.[12] Some anthropologists (and others), too, claim that law is always slightly out of step with society, because of the duality of the statement and restatement of rights.

All four theories are appealing, and at least the first three seem *prima facie* plausible. Inevitably the growth, history, and the social, political and religious outlook of a society will have some influence on the legal rules. Likewise, it is easy to concede that law will to a considerable degree operate to secure existing interests and to reduce friction. That much of law reflects the economic advantage of the ruling class is also readily apparent. Yet once that has been said for all three theories, it must be emphasised that they try to impose a pattern that does not exist. None of the theories does or can take account of the great extent to which legal rules are unsatisfactory for the society in which they operate and even for the ruling élite. The accuracy of the theories must be tested against the social facts, not by their intellectual neatness.

Elsewhere I have tried to show that to a very marked degree Western law has been and is out of step with the needs and desires of society.[13] Law, the argument was, in most places at most times has not developed and does not develop in a rational or responsive way, adapting easily to changing circumstances. This divergence is not to be attributed to ignorance—indeed the illustrations I used were of instances where the legal rule, principle or institution was inefficient for its purpose in satisfying the needs of the people or the will of the rulers, and where a better rule could be devised; and where both the inefficiency and the possibility of considerable improvement were known but not acted upon. It would be indecent to repeat the evidence adduced. But as an illustration I will give one example—which could be often repeated—from one system. The example has to be a broad one and treated systematically, and the system must be one of the most celebrated and respected.

A society is, of course, not monolithic but consists of various classes and groups with sharply conflicting interests. Even within a group the interests of the various individuals may differ greatly. Yet it should not be thought that the law that results for society is simply a patchwork of rules some of which suit the whole society, while others reflect the power of the various groups and suit them. It is possible to demonstrate that in important areas of law fundamental rules benefit neither the society as a whole nor particular groups; such rules may exist, detrimental to, or inconvenient for, the society, and be actively wanted by no one.

(III)

The example chosen is the Roman system of contracts. This has been very much admired, but even in its fundamental structure it contained grave defects that continued for century after century. Thus, the oldest and most basic contract was the *stipulatio*, which existed as early as the middle of the fifth century B.C. It was a contract that required formalities. The parties had to be present together, the promisee asked the other if he promised to give or do whatever it might be, and the promisor promised, using the same verb. No witnesses and no writing were required for the validity of the contract. *Stipulatio*, that is to say, was very simple in its form. Formalities required for the validity of a contract have various functions, two of which relate to evidence. Thus, formalities indicate to the parties themselves that they are entering a contract, and at the same time provide proof to the world at large both of the existence and of the terms of the contract. Of these two functions the latter is by far the more important, yet it is not at all fulfilled by the formalities for the Roman *stipulatio*. It is a grave weakness for a contract to need formalities for its creation that, however, go no way to prove the existence of the contract. People will—as Romans did—enter into the contract relying on the formalities only to find that when a dispute arises no evidence of the contract is available. This weakness in *stipulatio* was never really cured, although recording the stipulation in a document became so common that modern scholars discuss whether *stipulatio* had become a written contract by the third century A.D.

Probably *stipulatio* arose in circumstances in which the absence of the requirement of witnesses or of writing did not matter, either because the promise at first gave rise to no civil action but involved an oath calling a god to witness, or because it was a guarantee given in court procedure that a party to an action would appear on the due day and hence the promise was in fact always public. What is surprising is that once *stipulatio* had emerged as an independent private law contract this obvious defect in the formalities continued so long unchanged.

The true Roman written contract, the so-called literal contract, suffered from the same weakness: the formalities that were necessary to create the contract were not sufficient to prove its existence. The contract was made by entries of a particular type in the creditor's account books. Naturally enough there was a contract only if the debtor agreed, but the entries provided no evidence of this agreement, and the evidence had to be supplied in some other way. The contract was shorter-lived than the stipulation, but here again the defect was never remedied.

Even when we turn to one of the most famous Roman legal inventions, the consensual contracts, that is contracts whose validity depends solely on the agreement of the parties, we find gross flaws. One of the great merits of these contracts is that they can be made between parties who are not present together and who send a letter or messenger. Of the consensual contracts sale was the most important and probably the oldest, and was in existence by the late third century B.C. But originally and for a long time thereafter there was no guarantee inherent in the contract that the object sold was free from hidden defects or that the seller would transfer to the buyer a title good enough to stand up against the claims of other people. If a seller delivered, in good faith, the thing sold to the buyer, and at that stage another person proved he was owner and so gained control of the thing, the buyer had no redress against the seller on the contract of sale. If the buyer wished to be protected against the possibility of hidden defects and eviction—and he would in any important sale—then he had to take specific guarantees. This could be done only by *stipulatio*, which required that the parties be present together, hence effectively the contract of sale could not be made at a distance by making use of a letter or messenger. Thus the advantage of consensuality could not be exploited to anything like the full extent. Moreover, since the buyer had to draft his own guarantee (acceptable to the seller) flaws in legal expression could easily thwart his intention. Only very gradually was the position improved. The earliest traces of a built-in warranty—and even that protection is unsatisfactory—date from around the beginning of the second century A.D., at least three centuries after the creation of the contract. Yet we know from other branches of Roman law that the jurists were familiar with and capable of handling the idea of an inherent guarantee.

The final major class of Roman contracts is of those that are created by delivery. There were four such contracts and one of these, deposit, need never have existed since its scope was adequately covered by the earlier consensual contract of mandate. This unnecessary multiplication of types of contract would make it more difficult to see the underlying common factors in contract, and it is perhaps not surprising that the Romans never developed a general law of contract but only individual contracts. A further contract that came into being by delivery was *mutuum*, loan for consumption, and here the relevant action known as *condictio* did not permit the recovery of any interest on the loan. If interest was wanted—as it would be in any commercial transaction—a *stipulatio* was again necessary. The action on the *stipulatio* was also the *condictio*, which was an abstract action in the sense that the pleadings did not set out the ground of the claim. The *stipulatio* might be for the interest alone, in which case if the borrower failed to repay he had to be sued by two separate *condictiones*, one on the *mutuum*, one on the *stipulatio*; or the *stipulatio* might cover both the return of the amount loaned and the interest, in which case only one *condictio* —on the *stipulatio*—would be needed. It is easy to believe that in these circumstances *mutuum* as a commercial contract would be uncommon. Yet if the whole transaction was covered by one *stipulatio* a serious difficulty might arise. A feature of the *condictio* is that if the plaintiff overclaimed he lost his whole case and he was not allowed to renew his action. Now, at times it would be easy to prove the fact of the loan, less easy to show the existence of the *stipulatio* for interest. If the plaintiff sued for principal plus interest and could only show that there had been a loan he would lose entirely and not even be able to recover the sum he had lent.

More bizarre still is the failure of the Romans to develop a contract of barter until the first century A.D., at the very earliest. Even well into the following century, any such contract—if one existed—was so unsatisfactory that one of the two famous schools of jurists argued unsuccessfully that barter fell within the scope of the contract of sale. So eager were they for this recognition of barter as sale that they produced a text of Homer that, they erroneously claimed, showed a transfer of goods for money being treated like any other transfer of goods for goods.[14]

The examples we have looked at in this section all concern the most fundamental aspects of the contractual system but it would have been easy—though, I believe, unnecessary—to multiply examples of defects by looking at specific weaknesses within individual contracts. What concerns us here is that grave defects existed in the famous Roman contractual system and lasted for centuries. One cannot explain this away simply by saying that law reacts sluggishly.

The defects are of various types. Some involve problems, which can be avoided by taking pains that should not have been necessary. Others make the law unduly complicated. Others again create difficulties that are insurmountable—such as the practical impossibility of making a valuable contract of sale at a distance. All have in common that they remove law from the easy understanding of non-lawyers, that they cause unnecessary expense, and that they are actively beneficial to no one class, to no particular group, and certainly not to any governing élite. Lawyers alone might be thought to benefit consistently and yet there is no evidence for a powerful class of lawyers at Rome who would benefit directly from inefficient law. Not one of the defects can be attributed to something deep in the Roman psyche. The needs and desires of neither the people as a whole nor of the ruling élite were met or helped by any of the aspects of contract that we have considered.

Similar investigations of other branches of law in Roman law and in other systems such as English law would also show a wide divergence of law from the needs and desires of society.[15] The reader need only be reminded of the traditional horrifying complexities of English real property law—described by Oliver Cromwell as 'a tortuous and ungodly jumble'. It was 1975 (as a result of the 1925 legislation) before the English Chief Land Registrar could declare that compulsory registration of land for the whole of England and Wales was in sight, yet the benefits of compulsory registration had been known for centuries—in 1535, indeed, Henry VIII had a bill prepared for compulsory registration of conveyances. The feudal system of tenure—complicated enough to baffle and defeat experienced conveyancers—retained great legal effect and consequence until 1925 despite its manifest economic absurdities and although it did not serve any particular social need. As for the law of torts, the Faulks Committee in 1975 recommended the abolition of the distinction between libel (a defamatory statement cast in a form not purely transitory) and slander (oral and unrecorded words or gestures), which they attributed to historical accident and which they declared 'renders this part of the law unreasonable and unnecessarily complicated and refined, carrying a host of rules and exceptions, derived partly from precedent and partly from statute, which are illogical, difficult to learn, and in certain applications, it must be added, unjust'. In 1843 a similar recommendation was made by a select committee of the House of Lords but was never acted on. Many academic writers since have condemned the distinction and none seems to have supported it. The Porter Committee, which reported in 1948, declared that the law was 'arbitrary and illogical'. The majority, however, preferred to retain the distinction, giving one argument, without any evidence in favour, and admitting that in Scotland the distinction was not made and no serious disadvantages had been suffered.

English law in fact shows that criminal law may diverge just as much from the needs of society as does private law. One example from many may suffice here. The famous 'benefit of clergy' from the fourteenth century until its abolition in 1827 had a deep and grotesque influence on the shape of English criminal law. Even afterwards some of its peculiar effects remained. Thus, its existence resulted in the rebuttable presumption (abolished in 1925) that, if a married woman in the presence of her husband committed a crime of a certain type, her husband had coerced her; it also appears to have led judges to develop the doctrine in murder of 'constructive malice aforethought' which was abolished in 1957. Even today the question put by the judge to a person found guilty, namely whether he has anything to say before sentence is passed, is a survival; that is the moment when previously 'benefit of clergy' was claimed.

(IV)

The causes of this divergence are best analysed in terms of the creators of law. Law makers can be roughly divided into two groups; first, the legislators, who would include the popular assemblies, higher magistrates such as praetors, the Emperors of ancient Rome, and the Sovereign in Parliament in modern Britain; secondly, the interpreters of law, such as the jurists of Rome, judges in Britain, and university professors of law in France and Germany. The law-making powers of the legislators tend to be very much greater than those of the interpreters who, in some systems, are in theory not supposed to make law at all but only to find it.

The legislators for the most part are charged not only with making law but with governing. Their office is basically political in function, only secondarily legal. As a result it frequently happens that the legislators are just not interested in much of law—especially private law—or in law reform. Even if they are interested, pressure of other business, inflation, balance of trade, foreign relations, will often leave no time for thinking about law reform. Moreover, it is a feature of, for instance, British parliamentary life that the law reform considered by Parliament often does not reach the Statute Book because there is not enough time to go through all the formalities of legislating. One example will suffice. After a government committee on defamation had reported, a Defamation Bill was introduced in 1952, which had as clause 11 the provision that in order to mitigate damages a defendant might produce facts relevant to the plaintiff's character. This clause was dropped solely because there would not otherwise have been time to finish the Third Reading of the Bill on the due date. A notorious case of 1961, *Plato Films Ltd. v. Speidel*,[16] showed how needed such a clause was, and this led to the introduction of the Freedom of Publication Bill in 1966. But this failed to become law because no time was found for a second reading. Now a further committee on defamation, the Faulks Committee, have again recommended such a reform.[17]

The political rôle of the legislators inhibits law reform in yet another way. Frequently, legislators are politically chosen and they have to be concerned about their future, hence they may hesitate to introduce legislation that, needed and welcome as it might be overall, could offend even a small number of their supporters. Thus, in Britain governments do not introduce legislation on divorce reform. That is left to private members' bills, and the time allotted for these is very limited. It is highly significant that the Emperor Augustus, secure in his power, legislated extensively on marriage and divorce (and other family matters), whereas in the immediately preceding two centuries—the most fertile period for legal development in the world's history—no attempt was made by elected officials such as the praetors (who had extensive powers for legal development) to change anything in these fields.

Legislation, when it occurs, is itself often not the best that can be devised for the society. Frequently a carefully drafted bill is modified in the course of debate and an unsatisfactory compromise may emerge. Again much legislation is a 'gut reaction' to some particular event. Although the resulting law may well correspond to what was wanted at that moment, it may be very unsatisfactory in the long term. Yet once the law has been promulgated, factors such as those described above may prevent its modification for a very long time to come. Likewise a pressure group may push through legislation that is far from beneficial to the society as a whole or to the ruling élite. Circumstances may change, the pressure group may no longer exist, but the law continues. Again, private factors in the life of members of the ruling élite may result in legislation that meets the particular short term desires but that grossly ignores general needs. Such rules may then continue in force for centuries after the disappearance of the particular need. Let me give two examples. In A.D. 49, the Roman Emperor Claudius wished to marry his brother's daughter, Agrippina. Marriage between uncle and niece was prohibited and was regarded as incestuous but the senate passed a decree permitting marriage with a brother's daughter. Marriage with a sister's daughter remained void. This distinction corresponded to nothing in the Roman psyche. Yet even after the deaths of Claudius and Agrippina the law remained unchanged for virtually three centuries until a rescript of Constantius and Constans, of A.D. 342, made marriage with a brother's daughter once again illegal, and introduced the death penalty for incest between uncle and niece.[18] Secondly, King Henry VIII of England, being very short of money, sought to increase his revenues by the Statute of Uses, 1536. The Statute of Wills of 1540 provided a simpler and more effective protection for the royal feudal incidents with the result that there was no longer any strong reason to insist on the enforcement of the spirit of the Statute of Uses, and in any event the royal finances improved. But the Statute of Uses was passed with no real concern for other land-holding interests and its main effect was to block for a very considerable time the extremely popular device known as the 'use', which was the forerunner of the trust, one of the greatest creations of English law. There was no subsequent legislation to develop the use, and only gradually did lawyers invent to that end suitable dodges, which were acceptable in the Equity courts.

Of course, most legislation does meet a need of the society as a whole or of an important group.[19] What must be stressed above all is the longevity of legal rules and their power to survive long after any need has disappeared and they are out of step with anything that can be actively desired by the society or any forceful group.

(V)

The other law makers are those I have designated as the interpreters of law, such as the jurists of ancient Rome and the judges of modern Britain. Among lawyers, the interpreters tend to form a distinct, separate élite, with great prestige. In general, their law-making powers are limited, especially in theory, but the more the legislators fail to keep the law in harmony with society the greater the responsibility thrust on the interpreters. But the legislators do not give the interpreters power to change the law drastically, a fact that shapes the reforms they make. One should, however, beware of underestimating the law-making powers of the interpreters, especially where the legislators show little interest in private law. Thus, the greatest single determining factor on the shape of law in the modern world has been Roman law through its Reception in Western Europe, the transplanting of the law of European powers to their colonies, and then, with the advent of modern European codes, the wider dissemination of Roman law through their influence on codification, especially in South America and Asia. Yet the Reception of Roman law in Europe, which was a slow process taking centuries, was very largely the work of interpreters rather than of the legislators.

The restriction on the law-making powers of the interpreters determines in the first place the kind of argument that can be used to justify the interpretation. Only some kinds of argument are respectable, above all argument by analogy from existing legal rules in a similar context, or from authority, such as precedent in one's own system or an opinion expressed for another system that is held in esteem. These arguments have in common that they are of necessity backward looking. Even if the interpreter is in fact bringing about a legal revolution he must justify it with such arguments. This can only reinforce conservative tendencies, and it is notorious that the pace of reform by interpretation is slow.

Secondly, the interpreters have usually no power to abolish existing rules, however unsuitable they may be. To mitigate the worst effects of these the interpreters have to find exceptions or invent new principles, which they impose on the rules. The net result is a legal scaffolding, sometimes of horrendous complexity, which can be understood only by the specialist lawyer. Law becomes remote from the understanding of the people most affected. More than that, because of its haphazard growth the scaffolding can scarcely ever cope with all the tasks it should, and in its turn it becomes rigid and in need of reform. But the very existence of the scaffolding makes a general reform more difficult, since an overall view of the law and the problems is obscured for lawyer and layman alike.[20]

On a different level, the professional outlook of the interpreters, and also of the lawyers who aid the legislators, has a profound effect on the form that innovations take. But this topic is best left for the next chapter.

(VI)

This divergence of law from the needs of the people and their rulers enables us to draw some conclusions about the nature of law.

In the first place we must admit that there is no close, inherent, necessary relationship between law and the society in which it operates. Law cannot be said to be 'the spirit of the people'. Nor is it the inevitable result of existing material conditions. It should be noted that if many legal rules are not well suited to their society then it must also be the case that many rules which work tolerably well have likewise no intimate connection with the society. A very different rule might do just as well. In fact the longevity of legal rules coupled with the frequency of borrowing from another jurisdiction—indirectly the subject of the next chapter—means that only a minority of rules were created for the society in which they now operate.

Secondly, law does not emerge easily from the conditions of society and indeed does not develop easily at all. The pull of inertia is very great.

Thirdly, the great extent and deleterious effects—especially economic effects—of unsatisfactory law are not so obvious as one might expect. Otherwise reform would be forthcoming. This can only mean that the effect of unsatisfactory legal rules on the well-being of the society and the happiness of individuals is considerably less than jurists like to imagine. Of course, some bad rules, such as those on divorce, may cause some people enormous anguish; but at any one time only a very small proportion of the people in a state will actually suffer from law that is out of step with general needs and desires.

Fourthly, neither society nor its ruling class is usually too interested in the state of law, especially of private law. Society finds it surprisingly easy to tolerate unsatisfactory law, and pressure on the legislature for reform is very limited. There is no great demand for the 'best law'.

To avoid misunderstanding it should perhaps be made explicit that the claim is not that there exists no connection between society and its laws, merely that to a very great extent society can and does make do with legal rules that are unsuitable, inappropriate, imperfect, even though the possibility of better law is very apparent.

(VII)

To end this chapter on a very different note. It is a striking feature of law, including the law of a territorial state, that despite all its power and its wide scope it does not directly invade all aspects of human activity. In some sensitive areas—which change from place to place and from time to time—there exists a principle that may be stated as 'Law keeps out'. In some of these areas there will in fact be legal rules, but when they are considered closely it will emerge that their message, too, is 'Law keeps out'. It will be remembered that law is only one agent of social control; religion and popular morality may be mentioned as others.

We are made most aware of the principle when, looking at a different system, we suddenly find legal rules in existence where for us the basic norm is 'Law keeps out'. Instances of this may be found in the Prussian code, the *Allgemeines Landrecht für die Preussischen Staaten* of 1794. The second title of part two concerns the rights and duties of parents, and provides *inter alia*:

s.61 Children owe both parents respect and obedience.

s.67 A healthy mother is under the obligation of suckling her child herself.

s.68 How long she must keep the child at the breast is determined by the father's decision.

s.69 He must, however, submit himself to the ruling of experts if the health of the mother or child would suffer from his decision.

s.76 If the parents are devoted to different religious confessions, then until the fourteenth year is complete, sons should be educated in the religion of the father, daughters in the religious confession of the mother.

s.77 Neither of the parents can bind the other, even by contract, to set aside these legal rules.

s.109 The settling of the future mode of life of sons depends in the first instance on the judgment of the father.

s.121 Children are bound in accordance with their strength to provide a helping hand to their parents and their business and trade.

s.122 But time necessary for their teaching and education should not be taken from the children in that way.

From such familial areas, today, in general, 'Law keeps out'. In twentieth-century Britain the classic instance of the principle is the immunity from liability of a trade union for tort or delict, and so on (ignoring the legislation of 1971, which was repealed in 1974). The basic message of law makers in the Trade Disputes Act, 1906, is that law and legal process are not suitable means to resolve conflicts in this area.

It might be argued that there is, of course, law on these matters, and that if a trade union is sued in tort or delict, or in contract for breach of a collective agreement at common law, the dispute will be resolved in that the union will win in the case. But, it might further be claimed, unregulated conflict is not inhibited since the immunity leaves legally unregulated conflict as the means of settling industrial disputes. The conclusion would therefore be that the function of the process here cannot be—and hence the essential function of a legal process cannot be—the resolution of a dispute with the specific object of inhibiting further unregulated conflict. There are two answers to this. The first is based on 'Law keeps out'. The effect of the law is that there should be no processes because law is not thought to represent a satisfactory way of dealing with these disputes in twentieth-century Britain. The second and less satisfactory answer is to stress that the specific object of the process involves inhibiting further unregulated conflict, not necessarily abolishing it; and that the dismal failure of the Industrial Relations Act of 1971 shows that the removal of trade union immunity causes further unregulated conflict.

The opposite tendency to 'Law keeps out' is also in evidence at times. The state may intervene determinedly to resolve disputes even though there is already in existence a highly controlled method of inhibiting conflict. For instance, in the past gentlemen whose honour was injured might have recourse to duelling, which was highly regulated. But states, jealous of their authority, have outlawed duelling and restricted legal recourse to a process.

7

Lawyers' Thinking and Legal Rules

(I)

One matter of fundamental importance for the relationship between law and society was mentioned but not stressed in the preceding chapter, namely that in any society where division of labour prevails the making of law is very largely in the hands of a specially trained group, the lawyers. Almost inevitably the interpreters of law are lawyers. The legislators, too, frequently include lawyers in their number—noticably true today above all in the U.S.A., in the House of Representatives and the Senate —but whether they do or whether they do not the legislators normally seek advice on the contents of their enactments from trained lawyers, and entrust to such specialists the drafting of their laws. This is as true of the rescripts of the later Roman Emperors as of the Acts of the modern British Parliament.[1]

Consequently, law has a flavour that is peculiarly due to trained specialists. To the extent that this is so, law will be the more remote from the people and the ruling élite as a whole. Inevitably, some law will reflect the economic self-interest of lawyers and also professional solidarity. But that is an aspect that need not be emphasised here. Rather, in this chapter I wish to consider some of the more general implications of the formation of law being largely in the hands of these trained specialists and to show how the dominating rôle of lawyers can affect the relationship between law and society. This central position of lawyers has, of course, been stressed by other writers. For Savigny, for instance, division of labour means that what previously in a society had been done in common becomes the preserve of a group. Jurists emerge, law becomes more scientific and becomes proper to the consciousness of the jurists, who in this regard represent the people. Law, in Savigny's view, now has a double life: as part of the life of the whole people, which it continues to be, and as a special and complex science in the hands of jurists. Thus, in Savigny's opinion, immense legal detail can emerge in an organic manner free from any real arbitrariness.[2] Similarly, the search for self-consistency, which Engels thought could be found in law and which obstructed law from being a faithful reflection of material conditions, can only be the work of a trained professional body of lawyers.

To demonstrate the phenomenon and its significance for law and society I propose to deal here with only one, but the most important, consequence of law being developed by lawyers, namely that law is frequently borrowed from elsewhere. Only specialists normally have enough knowledge of other people's law to make use of it for their own system. It can, of course, happen that a non-lawyer experiences and appreciates other law, but this occurs too rarely to account for the phenomenon of legal transplants.[3]

Naturally, the influence of lawyers on the shape of legal development is by no means restricted to borrowing legal ideas from elsewhere. But the phenomenon of borrowing shows more clearly than anything else the importance for legal rules of lawyers' training, contacts and habits of thought, as distinct from factors inherent in the life of the society; and from this phenomenon we can generalise as far as we need.

(II)

The major ingredient of most legal systems—Western systems at least—is what has been borrowed from elsewhere. This is not universally true: Roman law, above all, seems to have borrowed little. But in general, individual rules, whole branches of law, even the structure of the system, owe their existence to a former life elsewhere. For the general accuracy of this statement one need think only of the Reception of Roman law in Europe and its growth beyond, into South America, South Africa, Japan, Ethiopia, Turkey, Quebec, Louisiana and elsewhere, and of the spread of English common law into most English-speaking lands, into North America, Australia, New Zealand, and so on. Naturally enough, modifications are frequently made in the law at the moment of borrowing and later—different societies do require different things—but these alterations are surprisingly minor. One striking, but possibly inevitable, feature of major legal transplants is that the borrowing system very soon seems to lose awareness of the extent of the indebtedness. The borrowing may also be so indirect—for instance as a result of legal writers' knowledge of other systems being translated into a new practical approach—or so gradual—as in much of the Reception of Roman law in Western Europe—that the borrower was in fact never aware that so much had been taken over. A few examples will make plain some of the importance of borrowing.

The most fundamental division of law is into public law and private law. It is a division made in modern Western law and in Roman law, and seems to us inevitable. The law is so divided up for teaching purposes in university courses, in law books, whether written for students or for practitioners, and, in countries where the law is codified, in the various codes of law. But the inevitability is an illusion. The division is not much in evidence in, for instance, either ancient Greek law[4] or mediaeval law. Thus, the division is not apparent in works so diverse as the German *Sachsenspiegel* of the early thirteenth century or, in Scotland, in Balfour's *Major Practicks* in the early seventeenth century. In fact in the modern world the division is the result of Roman law influence, and is accordingly much more in evidence in the civil law than in the common law countries. What is really surprising and significant, however, is that no satisfactory theoretical basis for the distinction is made. The Romans were content with this very jejune definition at the very beginning of Justinian's *Institutes* (1.1.4):

> There are two branches of this discipline, public and private. Public law is that which is concerned with the condition of the Roman state, private that which belongs to the advantage of individuals.

Although at Rome the division had existed for a very long time (and Roman jurists had more or less ignored public law), this definition is not satisfactory. Apart from other considerations, many legal institutions were regarded by the Romans themselves from one angle as private law, from another as public law. For instance, *tutela*, guardianship, is always treated as part of private law but the Romans insisted it was a *munus publicum*, a public obligation. We would incline to treat the law of civil procedure as public law because its rules really determine how the power of judges should be exercised. The Romans—witness the discussion both in Justinian's *Institutes* and in the classical Gaius' *Institutes*—thought of it as private law. How it fits within the definition provided by Justinian is even more of a puzzle. Again, criminal law is thought of by us as public law, yet in Justinian's *Institutes*, which otherwise treats only of private law, it appears as the very last title and, at that, one headed 'De publicis iudiciis'. The basic problem is, of course, that all law (or, perhaps, virtually all law) is both public and private. In modern law the distinction between public law and private law is not always drawn in the same place as in Roman law yet still it is drawn. The theoretical difficulties in the distinction, however it is conceived, are stressed by modern writers.[5]

A very different example may be chosen from one specific contract, sale. The legal rules, as they exist and operate today in both civil law and common law countries, are very recognisably similar to those in the developed Roman law of the second century A.D. ('Civil law systems' are those on which the predominant influence has been Roman law, 'common law systems' use English law and its derivatives.) There are differences, of course, but those between Swiss and Roman law are scarcely greater than those between French law and Swiss law. What, above all, is marked is that the scope of the contract of sale—with all the rules that are inherent in the contract simply because it is a sale—has remained unaltered. Sale is a contract for the delivery of goods in return for a money price. It is therefore not the same contract as hire (of a thing), which is the temporary transfer of control of a thing for money: when the contract reaches its termination, the control of the thing reverts. Nor is sale the same as barter, which is delivery of goods for goods. To the modern Western jurist it seems self-evident that this must be so. Yet need it be? In Islamic law barter is treated as part of sale; money-changing, money for money, which would not be sale in Roman law is sale; and what for us is hire is there sale of a usufruct.[6] More interestingly, the Romans themselves were not always sure where the line should be drawn between sale and other contracts. Thus, we find in the second century B.C. what for us is the lease of winter pastures being treated as sale;[7] and even in the second century A.D. one of the two famous schools of jurists, the Sabinian, argued that barter should be included within the contract of sale.[8] Again in other matters, even apart from the scope of the contract, the law of buying and selling in, for instance, Scotland, as late as the second half of the sixteenth century on the eve of the Reception, would astonish anyone not a specialist in legal history. The applicable rules vary with the status of the parties, as burgesses, sons of a burgess, as foreigners, and so on, and on the nature of the things sold, such as herring, meat or clothes. Sale does not appear to be a consensual contract.[9] In law we are closer to the Romans than to our own ancestors of four centuries ago.

Foreign legal tradition is particularly important in the systematization of law. The influence here may be concealed but thereby works all the more powerfully. In a recent paper on 'Innovation in Nineteenth Century Contract Law', A. W. B. Simpson[10] stresses that until then it was not easy to formulate and identify the common law doctrine of contract. But he goes on to say:[11]

> When the late eighteenth and early nineteenth-century writers on contract set about the task of systematic exposition of the abstract principles of contract law they were engaged upon an enterprise which was new to the common law (for reasons essentially connected with the history of legal education) but old to the civilian tradition; they were trying to do what the civilians, the canonists and the natural lawyers had been doing for centuries. Hence for plagiaristic purposes they turned, as Bracton had done six centuries earlier, and St Germain three, to the written reason of the Romanist tradition as a source of analysis, categories, and organising conceptions in which the local common law could be presented and its *lacunae* filled with speculative and, hopefully, influential discussion.

He points out that English treatise writers of the nineteenth century married their knowledge of the common law to their knowledge of writers such as Pothier, Domat, Pufendorf and Grotius, and Roman law, and he continues:

> In contemporary treatises on English Contract law you will find little trace of this internationalism; the days of general jurisprudence are over and such works as Anson (in its modern form), Cheshire and Fifoot, Treitel, Sutton and Shannon, and Atiyah, which are now the staple foods of

students, and directly or indirectly the profession, only occasionally relieve their insularity with references to other common law jurisdictions; they hardly ever step outside the common law world. It has become the aim of a number of modern English legal writers to avoid incursions into both history and other legal traditions; English law is to be presented as capable of standing alone. But in this they conceal the historical origin of much of what they transmit as homespun law, just as they conceal too the historical source of the literary tradition in which they stand. Yet they curiously continue to present the law as consisting of rational principles which are merely illustrated by the cases; to this extent they maintained the natural law tradition.

The borrowing of systematics is even more obvious in civil law jurisdictions, where the contents of the civil codes correspond to the contents of Justinian's *Institutes*, although the final titles of the latter on actions and criminal law are excluded. The modern codes and the sixth-century students' elementary textbook deal with the same areas of law, the same set of problems, and in large part follow the same arrangement of subject matter. The contents of a modern civil code—and, even more significantly, the exclusions—have been dictated by the contents of an ancient legal textbook, and yet it is precisely this law that has been and largely still is regarded as 'the hard core, the true heart of the law'.[12]

(III)

When one seeks to explain the vast amount of borrowing and its extreme importance for legal development, perhaps the first thought to occur is that it is only natural; humans build on human experience. The invention of one man can be and is used by many, of whom some add improvements that in turn can be adopted by others. But then one has to admit, *pace* Montesquieu, that the rules of one nation are not so peculiar to it that they cannot serve elsewhere. More than that, one has to say that in this regard law develops on trust, perhaps by reason, but not really by any practical experience. For instance, when Justinian's *Corpus Juris Civilis* was again seriously studied, and lectures were given on Roman law in Bologna in the twelfth century, and the Reception gradually began, the auditors who were responsible for the adoption of Roman rules in their own country had no experience of how satisfactory the rules would be in practice. Moreover, neither had the professors, who did not even have any ancient Romans to enquire from. The sources themselves for the most part do not disclose whether the rules produced desirable results at Rome, since they are concerned only with what the law is, not with its effects. Traditionally, law books have set out the legal rules but not their social consequences. Likewise, when Scottish students studied in Holland in the seventeenth century and brought back Roman law they had neither practical experience of how these rules would work in Scotland, nor had they read in their books or heard in their lectures how well these rules suited Dutch society. In other words, in these and very many other instances what is borrowed is an idea, not experience. And the borrowers are legal experts who like the idea.[13]

From the standpoint of society there are economic reasons for borrowing. Whether a society is faced with a particular problem new to it or with the need to build up a satisfactory legal system, it is far less wasteful of human and material resources to look at what another society has done and borrow with necessary modifications than to think through all the difficulties afresh.

But possibly the main cause of borrowing lies in the need of authority for law. As has been maintained in previous chapters, law and the legal process must rest on authority that is recognised as such and obeyed as such. Otherwise neither law nor process will have any efficacy. But as a consequence both legislators and legal interpreters will seek to bolster the authority they already have by seeking for and finding further authority. Thus, as we shall see in the next chapter, in the ancient Mediterranean world legislators often claimed their laws came from a god. The legal interpreters, too, bolster their opinion by reference to those who have reached the same conclusion. So common was it for Roman jurists to list others who agreed with them that we find Cicero in the first century B.C. teasing the jurist Trebatius with the fact.[14] There is more in all this than the habitual scholarly method of supporting one's opinion by accumulating references to others who share it. In other fields, such as pure science, there are objective facts; the problem is to find them, explain them, and make the conclusions palatable. The opinion of other scholars does not affect the facts, but in making one's conclusions palatable it is helpful to show that others are in some measure of agreement. Law shares this use of authority. But in addition law is a human construct made by, and dependent for its very existence on, authority that is accepted. Legislators and legal interpreters alike borrow respected law both because for themselves it has some authority and because the persons to whom it is applied will accept it the more readily because of this additional authority. At times, indeed, foreign law is borrowed more because of its prestige than because of its quality. And lawyers even claim to borrow when they are not doing so.

(IV)

When foreign law is borrowed this is by no means always in the wake of a search for the most suitable law. To the question of the rôle of quality in borrowed law I shall return, but first I should like to discuss the two other important factors in the choice of the law to be adopted.[15]

The first of these factors is the accessibility of foreign law, which may be due either to the nature of the foreign legal sources or to history often unconnected with legal matters.

The accessibility of the sources means above all that they are written and in a form open to easy consultation. Into modern times Roman law was the most accessible law. Justinian's *Institutes*, written as a students' elementary textbook which had the force of law, gave (and still give) immediate insight into the basic principles of law. The *Digest* and *Code*, on the other hand, provided a treasury of examples not only of principles but of their application to individual cases. The *Digest* is particularly noteworthy in setting out abstractly the relevant facts of a problem, presenting and often explaining the decision. Matters that are irrelevant to the legal point but that might be important in an actual law suit, such as the names and social importance of the parties and the strength of the evidence for the alleged facts, are rigorously excluded. The law emerges clearly and succinctly.[16] This is in sharp contrast with a mediaeval English law report, where facts that are relevant and irrelevant to the law are both given, where counter-allegations of fact appear, where we have the names of the parties and information on their social standing, and where we have the judge's decision, which might be influenced by non-legal factors. Moreover, it is, and was, very difficult to find out what the law in general was since the reports of the cases in point are very scattered. In addition, before the days of textbooks it always was notoriously difficult to know what the principles of English law were. The Roman law sources were accessible also in a different way in that they were written in Latin,[17] a language known to all educated men.

The relative inaccessibility of English law has been mentioned. To a large extent its influence has been restricted to English colonies to which it was transplanted by conquest. The glaring exception to this is found in the United States of America after Independence. When new States and Territories were created they likewise came under the sway of the common law,[18] the reason being that English Law had become accessible to them, not through any official source but by means of William Blackstone's *Commentaries on the Laws of England*, which were based on his introductory lectures for students.[19] It has been pointed out that by 1776 nearly 2,500 copies were in use in America, of which 1,500 were the American edition of 1772.[20] At least 21 'straight' English editions were published in America, and from 1803 onwards at least 94 editions appeared with American notes. There were also at least 55 American abridgments for students. Significantly, the *Commentaries*, which in England was a four-volume work, was usually published in only two volumes in the States. A judge or attorney could easily carry the whole law round with him.

The great success story for legal transplantation in the nineteenth century is France. At first the expansion was due to Napoleon's armies. But after Napoleon's defeat the importance of the *Code civil* continued and spread even in countries that had not been occupied by French armies. Some territories accepted the *Code civil* in toto, others promulgated a code derived in large part from the French *Code*. One might mention, for instance, Belgium (which still retains the *Code civil*), Romania (whose code is simply a translation), the Italian code of 1865, Louisiana, the Dominican Republic (which adopted the *Code civil* in French in 1825, translated into Spanish only in 1884), Bolivia (whose code of 1831 is virtually a translation), Chile (and through the Chilean code French law spread its influence still wider in South America), and Egypt.[21] It has been suggested that this success was due to French prestige, but the main reason surely was the existence of the *Code civil*, which had no rivals and which made French law immediately accessible.

A territory's history may also determine which foreign law is accessible. Thus, in present day Africa a country's legal system will be largely based on the common law or civil law depending upon whether the country was a colony of Britain or of one of the Continental powers, respectively. This cannot surprise us: it has been claimed, for instance, that at Independence in 1957 there was no Ghanaian lawyer who had not received his basic legal training in England.[22]

The history of Scots Law provides us with a very different example. Until the fourteenth century English law was the main influence. Two-thirds of the earliest known Scottish law book, the *Regiam Majestatem*, derives from the English work attributed to Glanvill, *Tractatus de legibus et consuetudinibus regni Angliae*.[23] But the war between the two countries largely closed England to the Scots, who thereafter studied abroad. Even when the Scottish universities were founded—St Andrews was the first in 1413—law was either taught very badly or not taught at all. Scots continued to study law abroad; in the fifteenth century, mainly in Cologne, Louvain and North Italy; in the sixteenth century until the Reformation, in France as a result of the Auld Alliance; in the seventeenth and eighteenth centuries in Holland. The rise of modern Scots law is to be dated to the seventeenth century and, inevitably in view of this Continental, particularly Dutch, training, a great deal of Roman law is incorporated.[24] With the Union of the Parliaments of England and Scotland in 1707, the growth of trade between the two countries, and the Industrial Revolution, it was equally inevitable that English law would in time become the major influence.

A final example may be selected from North America. In the early nineteenth century both Quebec and Louisiana promulgated a civil code and both jurisdictions were undoubtedly civil law territories. Quebec certainly remains so despite some admixture of common law. But there have been very serious doubts whether in any real sense Louisiana can qualify as a civil law jurisdiction.[25] Many factors favoured the penetration of the common law into Louisiana,[26] but one of the most important was that English became overwhelmingly the language of the state and very little civil law material was available in that language.[27,28] Another factor was simply the absence in the formative years of judges and lawyers trained in civil law. The common law became accessible, civil law ceased to be so.

The second factor that—apart from an evaluation of quality—determines which system will be borrowed from is its prestige. It is not easy to assess this factor independently of accessibility and quality, but when more than one system is accessible it may help to determine which will be chosen, and it ensures that a rule will be borrowed without too detailed a consideration of the appropriateness of that rule. Given the nature of law and its intrinsic need for authority it is inevitable that prestige will play an important part in deciding whose rule is borrowed. But it is possible to exaggerate. Paul Koschaker, I think, goes too far in asserting that the reception of a legal system is not a question of quality, and that the 'receptibility' of a foreign legal system is much more a question of power, the result of—at least—a spiritual and cultural power position of the received law; and that this power position in turn is conditioned by the political power position, whether the power is still real or lives in the memory.[29] It is certainly true, as some of the examples already produced in this section indicate, that political power may determine that a particular legal system is the most accessible. Yet it would be difficult to maintain that the remembrance of the political power of the Romans was the dominant cause of the Reception of Roman law in Western Europe. The general high quality of the law and its accessibility through the *Corpus Juris* were more immediate factors. No doubt the belief that the Holy Roman Empire was a continuation of the Roman Empire would ensure there a more favourable attitude to Roman Law, but the Reception in the Holy Roman Empire was on the whole rather late. Of course, the possibility certainly exists that if it had not been for the prestige of ancient Rome, Roman law would not have been studied so attentively in the first place, but this would make the power position the *causa sine qua non* and not the *causa causans*. Likewise, in South America the prestige of France after Napoleon might have led people to regard French law with some respect, but there would have been no borrowing without the *Code civil*, which had no rival for accessibility. Significantly, the spread of French law was partly indirect. The Chilean code of 1865 belongs to the French family but is itself highly original; and it is this Chilean code that was copied by Ecuador and Columbia and served as a model in Uraguay and Argentina.

Law, though accessible, would not be borrowed unless it also had some merit. Likewise, the prestige of a foreign system is, at least in part, the result of quality. Law is borrowed because it is thought to be good law. This need not be stressed. What, however, needs to be emphasised is that the general quality of a foreign system can be so highly regarded—this is particularly true of Roman law—that it becomes difficult to see law except in that system's terms, and that inefficient rules will be borrowed along with satisfactory law. Again the very accessibility of one system may prevent a search for more appropriate law.

(V)

This chapter has been stressing the frequency of legal transplants, and this very frequency itself indicates that it is socially easy to accept foreign law. But to avoid any misunderstanding it should be made express that I am not claiming that any legal rule will suit every state and every society. The claim is merely that many rules, with or without variation, can be adopted by different societies. Naturally enough, in general a society will attempt to borrow only from foreign law rules and systematics that seem useful to it: wholly inappropriate law will not be borrowed.

But for legal rules or structure to be transplantable, it is not necessary that the lending and the borrowing system have the same political or economic organization. Rules and system can be transplanted into very different societies.[30] The Reception of Roman Law again provides the best illustration, whether the receiving society is a Germanic tribe in the fifth century, Southern France in the twelfth century, Catholic Spain, the various territories of Germany, whether Catholic, Lutheran or Calvinist, kingdoms, dukedoms or city states, or Protestant

Scotland in the seventeenth century. Certainly some institutions were never received at all and others underwent profound modification, but legal ideas are eminently transferable. Indeed, since in any one territory of reasonable size, say England, geographical conditions can vary greatly from densely populated cities to lonely mountains, and the population may be equally diverse—rich, poor, university trained, illiterate, Conservative, Marxist, Catholic, Hindu—one would expect that successful rules especially of private law would not be too closely associated with any one particular environment. Likewise, individual foreign legal rules may be transferred into a system constructed on very different principles. One example may stand for all. Feudal land ownership is vastly different from the absolute ownership of land known to Roman law. Yet this did not prevent countries like Scotland taking over the Roman rules of rustic praedial servitudes, that is burdens, such as right of way or drawing water, which are imposed on land in favour of neighbouring land in such a way that the obligation and the benefit are seen as attached to the land and transfer with it, and not as attached to the individual owners of the land.

A particular type of massive transplant is the voluntary adoption of a Western-style civil code by an economically underdeveloped nation with the deliberate intention of helping or forcing that country into the 'modern world'. Famous examples are Japan at the end of last century, Turkey in 1926, and Ethiopia in 1960. The civil code of Ethiopia is, in fact, not even the work of Ethiopians but of the French comparatist, René David. Some modern scholars have emphasised that in such cases the law may remain 'law in books' rather than 'law in operation'. The truly surprising thing, however, would be if the new law become operational overnight. The difficulties for this kind of transplant are not just those of changing social behaviour or ordering it in terms of the new law. The new law may scarcely be accessible because of the illiteracy of the people to whom it applies and the lack of satisfactory training facilities for judges and lawyers. In addition the state administration facilities may also be too underdeveloped to cope.[31] A delay in the code's becoming fully operational is not to be taken as meaning that the transplant has been rejected. It should be remembered that the Reception of Roman law—admittedly not imposed—was a slow process extending over centuries. What evidence there is indicates that in Turkey and Ethiopia the civil codes have achieved some degree of success, and that greater is to be expected.

(VI)

The great extent of legal borrowing and the ease with which it is achieved are very revealing for the nature of law. We see above all that legal rules and even the structure of a system are not closely bound to a country or society. Legal ideas transport easily to very different geographical, political, social and economic conditions. We also see that much of a society's law is tied to the thought of trained lawyers who use foreign ideas creatively, with no (necessary) experience, however, of how the foreign rules worked in practice.

In this and the preceding chapter I have been arguing that many rules of law are inappropriate for the society in which they operate, and that the rules arise less out of the particular conditions of society than from lawyers' knowledge, especially of what is done elsewhere. It will follow from this that many rules that are not inappropriate are also not particularly appropriate. Others, of course, will be very appropriate. Society has the ability to tolerate a great deal of law that is not the best that can be devised for that society, and knowledge of the deficiencies does not automatically cause intolerance. It appears that to a considerable extent what matters more is that there are rules than that the rules are the best suited for that society.[32]

If the argument is correct it should mean that it is not necessarily very important for society that a judge in a lawsuit get his law right (in the sense that the law in the decision results from the application of accepted types of legal reasoning, with proper use made of authority and analogy, from the legal rules and principles to the facts that are treated as relevant). It is important that the attempt be made to get the law right (or cynicism will ensue), and that the decision be acceptable. But what is of significance is that the law best suited for a society's needs is by no means inevitably that which exists in the society, and, to the extent that it is not, the expenditure of great effort in a law suit to achieve the legally correct result may be a misuse of resources. (It may be remarked that there is something rather bizarre in the contrast between the great effort expended in, say, the United Kingdom to get the correct legal result in a particular law suit and the relative lack of effort to ensure that the legal rule is the best possible.)

8

Respect for Law

(I)

Even without the argument in chapter 5 that law or a legal system not backed by force may still command obedience, we could have taken it for granted that obedience to law is not necessarily solely dictated by the force that backs the law. Individual legal rules are also obeyed or observed for psychological or social reasons: for instance, because the particular rule corresponds to one's own system of values, or because (even if one does not value the rule for its own sake) compliance brings rewards in the shape of preserving a particular social relationship.[1]

Psychological reasons for observing particular rules, however powerful these reasons may be, will not be discussed here. Rather, we will look very briefly at a psychological phenomenon that is wider in its general implications, namely respect for the law *as such*. Respect for law because it is law means, on the one hand, that we can envisage legal systems (though not of a nation state) which are not backed by force; on the other, that (for instance, in a nation state) the great extent to which law's validity depends on force is masked.

The importance of respect for law because it is law is, I believe, self-evident, but it is also clearly demonstrated by a number of factors, some of which may be looked at here under four headings: first, the awareness of the law makers that they should give their laws the appearance of great authority; secondly, the treatment of law-making by many law makers themselves as an occupation of the highest value; thirdly, the persistent idea that human rules that produce results regarded as unjust cannot possibly be law; fourthly, the frequency of legal transplants. Naturally, the first two sets of factors shade into one another. We will be concerned not with factors which show that law is worthy of respect but factors which either demonstrate that law is thought to be worthy of respect or derive from such feelings of respect.

(II)

Law makers' awareness that their law-making should have the appearance of great authority is at its most obvious in the claims common in the Ancient World that laws were created either by men appointed to that task by a god or inspired by a god, or were even the work of a god himself.

One of the earliest known codes of law, of king Lipit-Ishtar for Sumer and Akkad in the earlier part of the nineteenth century B.C., was divinely inspired by Enlil, the storm god and chief executive of the pantheon: 'then I, Lipit-Ishtar . . . [estab]lished [jus]tice in [Su]mer and Akkad in accordance with the word of Enlil'.[2] The epilogue of Hammurabi's Code of about a century and a half later proclaims:

> I, Hammurabi, am the king of justice,
> to whom Shamash committed law.
> My words are choice; my deeds have no equal;
> it is only to the fool that they are empty;
> to the wise they stand forth as an object of wonder.[3]

Shamash was the sun god and the god of justice.

A different yet related claim is made in the *Iliad* for Agamemnon. Nestor speaks:

> Most glorious son of Atreus, Agamemnon, king of men,
> with thee will I begin and with thee make an end,
> for that thou art king over many hosts and to thee
> Zeus hath vouchsafed the sceptre and judgments, that
> thou mayest take counsel for thy people.[4]

Here the claim is not that a god inspired Agamemnon's judgments but that Zeus gave Agamemnon the right to make judgment. The respect is not that due to law made or directly inspired by a god but that due to law made by a man appointed by a god to that end. We are this time looking at the law not from the point of view of the law maker but of, as it were, a customer. Obviously in a very important sense the fact that the law was made by a man diminishes the respect due to it, but in an extremely practical sense the change may actually increase the respect demanded for law. If law is admittedly made by a man and not a god, one need not be surprised if it is not wholly just; yet if the man is divinely appointed to that task then the judgment, though unjust, ought not to be challenged.

Diodorus Siculus records laws given by gods to men: Hermes to the Egyptians with Mneves as intermediary, Zeus to the Cretans through Minos, Apollo to the Spartans through Lycurgus, the Good Spirit to the Getae through Zarathustra, Jehovah to the Jews through Moses. Diodorus says that the intermediaries made such a claim

> either because they believed that a conception which would help humanity was marvellous and wholly divine, or because they held that the common crowd would be more likely to obey the laws if their gaze were directed towards the majesty and power of those to whom their laws were ascribed.[5]

In a similar, but possibly rather more credulous, vein is Dionysius of Halicarnassus' report of King Numa of Roma, who was allegedly aided by the nymph Egeria:

> But those who banish everything that is fabulous from history say that the report concerning Egeria was invented by Numa, to the end that, when once the people were possessed by a fear of the gods, they might more readily pay regard to him and willingly receive the laws he should enact, as coming from the gods. They say that in this he followed the example of the Greeks, emulating the wisdom both of Minos the Cretan and of Lycurgus the Lacedaemonian.[6]

The most instructive case is the bestowal of the Ten Commandments on the Israelites, where we are given surrounding information. God told Moses that if the Israelites would keep his covenant he would make them his holy nation. Moses reported to his people, who agreed. God then told Moses that the people should purify themselves, and that God would descend upon Mount Sinai on the third day in the sight of the people. But Moses was to put barriers round the mountain and anyone who touched the mountain was to be killed. In due course the people gathered round the mountain, which smoked. Whenever Moses spoke God answered in a peal of thunder. Moses climbed up the mountain and God told him to go down and warn the people not to force their way up or many would perish. Eventually, God gave Moses the Commandments. What interests us here above all, in the context of respect for law, is precisely that *before the laws were issued* Moses had to discover from the people whether they would be obedient, and in order to receive the laws the people had to purify themselves.[7] (A cynic might notice that only a few weeks at the most before this occurrence Moses' father-in-law told him that it was too wearing for Moses to spend all day hearing and settling disputes, that he should instruct the people in the law and teach them how to behave; moreover, he should appoint officers to sit as a permanent court. Moses did make such appointments, and the permanent court heard simple cases and brought difficult ones to Moses.[8]) Times change, it no longer seems appropriate to claim that new law is directly given by a god, and yet the respect still displayed towards the Ten Commandments owes much to belief in their divine authorship.

Under the same heading, that law should be clothed with the appearance of great authority, we can list some phenomena of contemporary law. For an English-speaking audience we need only call attention to the wigs and gowns worn by judges and barristers or advocates in court, the whole ceremonial of the trial, complete until recently, with trumpets, all adjuncts to increase the respect felt for the proceedings. We might also mention the offence of contempt of court, which is at least as much concerned with behaviour that offends the dignity of the court as with behaviour intended to pervert the course of justice. Judges are rightly known for their promptitude in dealing with any affront to their dignity. For contempt of court, it will be recalled, the punishment may be a sentence of imprisonment of indeterminate length.

(III)

Under our second heading—the treatment of law-making by law makers as an occupation of the highest value—it will be enough to look at the phenomenon of codification of law by leaders who also show outstanding talents in another field.

It is a striking fact that great military leaders, despots, and statesmen have been active in codifying law. Thus, in the preceding section we came across Lipit-Ishtar, who claimed in the prologue to his Code to have 'procured the freedom of the sons and daughters of Nippur, the sons and daughters of Ur, the sons and daughters of Isin, the sons and daughters of Sumer and Akkad upon whom slaveship had been imposed';[9] Hammurabi, famed as a conqueror—although recent research suggests his reputation is exaggerated;[10] and Moses, who led the Israelites out of bondage in Egypt. To them we must add for the Roman Republic Julius Caesar and Pompey the Great, both of whom, unsuccessfully, planned codifications.[11] Justinian, whose great codification, now known as the *Corpus Juris Civilis*, spread Roman law throughout the world, ruled the Byzantine Empire from 527 to 565 and reconquered Africa, Italy and part of southern Spain. The Prussian *Allgemeines Landrecht* of 1794 emerged from the direct initiative of Frederick the Great, who in 1749 had painted the ideal picture of a complete code in his *Dissertation sur les raisons d'établir ou d'abroger les lois*. The French *Code civil* of 1804, often called the *Code Napoléon*, needed the energy of the First Consul to bring it to completion.

Naturally, the prestige of these leaders would heighten regard for their codes. But much more is involved. It is significant for their attitude to law that they did not want simply to reform the law but to codify and systematise it. What matters most here is how these men regarded their codes: in some cases we have explicit and direct evidence. Moses claimed his as the work of God. Immediately after the passage quoted from the epilogue to his code, Hammurabi proceeds:

> If that man heeded my words which I wrote on my stela,
> and did not rescind my law,
> has not distorted my words,
> did not alter my statutes,
> may Shamash make that man reign
> as long as I, the king of justice;
> may he shepherd his people in justice!
>
> If that man did not heed my words which I wrote
> on my stela,
> and disregarded my curses,
> and did not fear the curses of the gods,
> but has abolished the law which I enacted,
> has distorted my words,
> has altered my statutes,

effaced my name inscribed (thereon),
and has written his own name,
(or) he has commissioned another (to do so) because
of these curses—
as for that man, whether king or lord,
or governor or person of any rank,
may mighty Anum, the father of the gods, who
proclaimed my reign,
deprive him of the glory of sovereignty,
may he break his sceptre, may he curse his fate!

May Enlil, the lord, the determiner of destinies,
whose orders cannot be altered,
who made my kingdom great,
incite revolts against him in his abode which
cannot be suppressed,
misfortune leading to his ruin!
May he determine as the fate for him a reign of woe,
days few in number, years of famine,
darkness without light, sudden death!
May he order by his forceful word the destruction
of his city,
the dispersion of his people, the transfer of his kingdom,
the disappearance of his name and memory from the land!

And more in the same vein. Justinian, in his turn, states at the beginning of the *Constitutio Deo Auctore*:

> Governing, under the authority of God, our empire which was delivered to us by His Heavenly Majesty, we prosecute wars with success, we adorn peace, we bear up the frame of the State, and we so lift up our minds in contemplation of the aid of the omnipotent Deity that we do not put our trust in our arms, nor in our soldiers, nor in our leaders in war, nor in our own skill, but we rest all our hopes in the providence of the Supreme Trinity alone, from whence proceeded the elements of the whole universe, and their disposition throughout the orb of the world was derived. 1. Whereas then there is in all things nothing found so worthy of respect as the authority of enacted law, which disposes well things both divine and human, and expels all iniquity, and yet we find . . .

And Napoleon:

> My glory is not to have won forty battles, for the defeat of Waterloo will destroy the memory of as many battles. But what nothing will destroy, what will live eternally, is my Civil Code.[12]

These leaders show that, in their view, law, and particularly their law, is of supreme importance for the well-being of the State.

It should not be forgotten that we are concerned here with factors which show that law is treated with respect, not with factors which show that law deserves to be treated with respect, and we need not discuss the quality of the law mentioned in this and the preceding section. What matters here is that the eminent respectability of good law appears to be a belief of the great legislators themselves.

(IV)

The concept of Natural Law also reveals the enormous respect which is thought due to law. Natural Law theories fall into two main types: those that claim Natural Law is law established by God and those that claim Natural Law is right reason or the Law of Reason.

To taste the flavour of such theories it will be enough to give some slightly abbreviated quotations from Hugo Grotius, *De Iure Belli ac Pacis*, 1.1.10.[13]

> 1) The law of nature is a dictate of right reason, which points out that an act, according as it is or is not in conformity with rational nature has in it a quality of moral baseness or moral necessity; and that, in consequence, such an act is either forbidden or enjoined by the author of nature, God.
>
> 2) The acts in regard to which such a dictate exists are, in themselves, either obligatory or not permissible, and so it is understood that necessarily they are enjoined or forbidden by God. In this characteristic the law of nature differs not only from human law, but also from volitional divine law; for volitional divine law does not enjoin or forbid those things which in themselves and by their own nature are obligatory or not permissible, but by forbidding

things it makes them unlawful, and by commanding things it makes them obligatory.

3) For the understanding of the law of nature, again, we must note that certain things are said to be according to this law not in a proper sense but—as the Schoolmen love to say—by reduction, the law of nature not being in conflict with them; just as we said above that things are called just which are free from injustice. Sometimes, also, by misuse of the term, things which reason declares are honourable, or better than their opposites, are said to be according to the law of nature, although not obligatory.

4) It is necessary to understand, further, that the law of nature deals not only with things which are outside the domain of the human will, but with many things also which result from an act of the human will. Thus ownership, such as now obtains, was introduced by the will of man; but, once introduced, the law of nature points out that it is wrong for me, against your will, to take away that which is subject to your ownership. Wherefore Paul the jurist said that theft is prohibited by the law of nature. . . .

5) The law of nature, again, is unchangeable—even in the sense that it cannot be changed by God. Measureless as is the power of God, nevertheless it can be said that there are certain things over which that power does not extend; for things of which this is said are spoken only, having no sense corresponding with reality and being mutually contradictory. Just as even God, then, cannot cause that two times two should not make four, so He cannot cause that that which is intrinsically evil be not evil.

This is what Aristotle means when he says: 'Some things are thought of as bad the moment they are named.' For just as the being of things, from the time that they begin to exist, and in the manner in which they exist, is not dependent on anything else, so also the properties, which of necessity characterize that being; such a property is the badness of certain acts, when judged by the standard of a nature endowed with sound reason. . . .

6) Sometimes nevertheless it happens that in the acts in regard to which the law of nature has ordained something, an appearance of change deceives the unwary, although in

> fact the law of nature, being unchangeable, undergoes no change; but the thing, in regard to which the law of nature has ordained, undergoes change. For example, if a creditor gives a receipt for that which I owe him, I am no longer bound to pay him, not because the law of nature has ceased to enjoin upon me that I must pay what I owe, but because that which I was owing has ceased to be owed. Thus Arrian in *Epictetus* reasons correctly when he says: 'To constitute an indebtedness it is not enough that a loan has been made; the obligation must remain as yet unsatisfied.' So if God should command that any one be slain, or that the property of any one be carried off, homicide or theft—words connoting moral wrong—will not become permissible; it will not be a case of homicide or theft, because the deed is done by authority of the Supreme Lord of life and property.
>
> 7) Furthermore, some things belong to the law of nature not through a simple relation but as a result of a particular combination of circumstances. Thus the use of things in common was in accordance with the law of nature so long as ownership by individuals was not introduced; and the right to use force in obtaining one's own existed before laws were promulgated.

In the *prolegomena* 11 to the same work Grotius claimed—also speaking in effect of Natural Law:

> What we have been saying would have a degree of validity even if we should concede that which cannot be conceded without the utmost wickedness, that there is no God, or that the affairs of men are of no concern to Him.

What must be stressed above all in the present context is that both types of Natural Law theories (in most versions) entail the idea that there exists an ideal law of supreme worth, which is essentially valid law, and that human rules which fail to reach some particular standard of excellence cannot count as law. But if one were then to ask why Natural Law theorists are so insistent that the rules and principles with which they are concerned are rules of law and not simply rules of morality, part of the answer would have to be that, aside from the force that backs law (which may back rules so evil that Natural Lawyers would deny them the status of law), there is an overriding obligation to obey law—which must mean all valid law—which is different in character from the obligation to behave morally. Since adherents of Legal Positivism tend to view Natural Lawyers as woolly-minded metaphysicians, it is worth noting that virtually all Natural Law doctrines have been intended to serve as a guide to practical conduct. Moreover, if one believes that the universe is a product of conscious design—whether the designer is God or a directing intelligence—then the 'laws of nature' are laws in rather more than a metaphorical sense: they have been laid down by a superior power. On this view, if for men to reach their full potential it be necessary that human societies should follow certain rules, then it follows that these rules have been prescribed for men by the superior power. Every creature, this argument goes on, has been created for a purpose, and is therefore obliged to conduct itself in the manner that will best enable it to attain the end of its creation.

Apart from theories of Natural Law, there is a widespread belief, as we have seen, that law reflects society or even its ideals. Legal rules are also considered to have a higher purpose, such as morality, justice, and freedom. In fact, it seems obvious to me that some have, some have not. Of those which have not, many are morally indifferent; some are evil. But the higher purpose of some rules is treated as pertaining to all. The point can be amply illustrated by two quotations—without comment—from the famous Roman jurist Ulpian, which are now placed at the beginning of Justinian's *Digest*:[14]

> A person who is about to give his attention to law (*ius*) ought first to know where the word *ius* comes from. Now it is so called from justice (*iustitia*); in fact, in accordance with the elegant definition of Celsus, law is the art of the good and the fair. 1. Of this art we are deservedly called the priests; for we worship justice and proclaim knowledge of the good and the fair, separating what is fair from what is unfair, distinguishing what is licit from what is illicit, wishing to make men good not only through fear of penalties but also by the appeal of rewards, striving after a true philosophy unless I am mistaken, not a false one.
>
> Jurisprudence is acquaintance with things divine and human, the knowledge of the just and the unjust.

Lastly in this context I should like to return for a moment to legal transplants. In most societies at most times—as I have already maintained—law develops primarily by borrowing from elsewhere a legal rule that seems appropriate. This overwhelming frequency of transplants is partly to be explained by the respect for legal rules. A legal rule exists; respect for it persuades a foreign jurist that it should be accepted also as the law of his country. Legal rules are treated as partaking of a degree of universality. Again, a further striking feature of legal rules, namely their longevity,[15] indicates a respect for what is not lightly to be changed.

(V)

We seem, in a way, to have presented ourselves with a paradox. Leaders distinguished in other fields turn to law-making as something that will win them great respect; it is their law-making that, they claim, will mark them out for eternal glory. Law appears as a supremely worthy human achievement. Yet law, I have been arguing, is essentially about order and is, almost inevitably, backed by violence and force. And the most typical law of all, that of a national state, is inconceivable without the backing of violence. 'Can law be evil?' asks an ancient philosopher and gives a negative reply.[16] That answer has been repeated through the centuries. Although we all know that states and other groups have made and will make wicked, immoral laws it nonetheless remains true that law and justice are intimately associated in men's minds. People feel peculiarly betrayed when a legal rule or process turns out to work injustice. A perpetual emotional spring of Natural Law theory is the belief that a man-made rule that is immoral cannot be law. Why? The rational answer is that law in this regard as in others is an organ of the state or group, hence discontent with law brings one into emotional conflict with the moral authority of the state; that law has an inherent tendency towards the moral; and that law is society's attempt to institutionalise justice.

Little need be said about the first of these three propositions. States as a matter of course claim moral authority and act as if their law deserves the greatest respect. How far this is a false reality, how far the rulers deliberately mislead the populace or are guilty of self-deception will vary from time to time and state to state. The idea of 'legitimate authority' in the Weberian sense is also relevant here.

Law has an inherent tendency towards the moral. To institutionalise disputes, to validate decisions on the disputes, to inhibit unregulated conflict, all these are moral objectives. Order is itself not a neutral quality but is a *prima facie* good. It may, of course, be claimed that some disputes arise because of a law, that an evil law may institutionalise disputes for an evil purpose, that law may validate an evil decision just as much as a good one, that the unregulated conflict which is inhibited is that of the forces of justice fighting against evil, and that the order created may be the enforced acceptance of a dictatorial monster. None of this can be denied or should be denied, but it means only that to institutionalise a dispute is not an unqualified absolute good. Few human activities are.

More to the point, most legal rules when they are made have no direct effect for good or ill upon the law makers personally; likewise in a process, the judge in most instances has no personal interest in the outcome. This is so even in a tyranny. The law maker or judge, faced with a choice in such a situation, will tend to choose justice (as he sees it) rather than injustice, the interests of society (as he sees them) rather than the reverse. He has no reason to favour injustice or the harm of society. Indeed, the reverse is true since such a choice might be creative of unrest and disorder, which cannot be actively desired for law. A vote for justice and the interests of society is a vote for order.

We must, however, be clear as to what is here meant by justice and morality. We are not talking in terms of an abstract theory known to and appreciated by only a few philosophers, but of what people feel and declare to be just whether or not they base themselves on any explicit theory. And the people whose moral views matter in this context are the people in the society or the ruling élite, not outsiders whose opinions are relevant only in so far as their outrage may have effects within the society (as by an invasion, or inciting rebellion, or upsetting the consciences of the local inhabitants).[17] Should the morality of the people be warped then so may be the morality of their law, but for the insider the law will here express practical morality.

But even in states that we would regard as most wicked the great bulk of the law may still appear to the outsider to be in accordance with morality. The reason is that the wickedness, whether induced by self-interest, or by religious or political ideology, will be reflected in only a few legal rules, though these may be very prominent. For instance, if a state practises extreme racial discrimination, forbidding intermarriage between the races, or expropriating one racial group, all this will have little effect on other aspects of the law of marriage, contract and property. The law makers will still make rules and the courts will still adjudicate on the minimum age for marriage, consents necessary for the marriage, financial arrangements between the spouses during the continuance of the marriage and at its end, divorce, and so on—all matters unaffected by the racist laws. And the rules and decisions will be based on principles accepted as moral by a wide circle of opinion, even outside the state.

But the morality in law is not the highest imaginable; law does not, for instance, impose a duty of brotherly love.[18] Indeed, even where a society believes in the virtue of acting carefully its law may impose liability only for deliberate wrongdoing. A fine example is provided by early Roman law where the guardian of a child or woman, the *tutor*, was liable only for fraud.[19] Yet, as the derivation of the word *tutor*—from the verb *tueri* 'to protect'—shows, the rôle of the guardian was understood to be looking after the ward's affairs.[20]

Law is also society's attempt to institutionalise justice. We need not linger over the fact that law courts are frequently officially entitled 'Courts of Justice', or that the term 'Minister of Justice' usually means the politician charged with the running of the law courts. But legal rules exist to institutionalise disputes and to validate the decisions in the process. What is usually prominent in a process is the judge's intention to reach an objective assessment of the legal issues presented to him, and where the dispute is between individuals or institutions not directly forming part of the state, the arbitral rôle of law is obvious, and the force or violence that backs the law and ensures that the judgment will be enforced is scarcely apparent. The state seems to hold the ring between the quarrelling parties and fixes fair rules. In a criminal trial, the force or violence backing the law is very obvious; and so it should be. It is a basic part of justice in common morality that retribution follows wrongs.

Nonetheless, it should again be stressed that law and justice have no inevitable connection, and that in no sense is the doing of justice an essential function of positive law, whether of the rules of law or of the legal process. Alas, the association of justice with law leads only too often to a view popular with politicians that if something is done in accordance with law then it is right, and no more discussion is required. Many of the world's greatest atrocities are committed legally.[21]

It may be, and I believe it is the case, that the reasons given above are not sufficient to explain the respect for law that does exist. Tentatively, I admit that I would be tempted by a proposition that man, like all social animals, has evolved his behaviour to a group pattern that sets a premium upon order. This means that distant ancestors who explored alternative behaviours were less successful in their evolution, and have failed to survive. Mechanisms, physical, psychological and institutional, which are conducive to order, have by definition a selective value whether they operate at a conscious or subconscious level. Law, which is essentially about order, is such an institutionalised mechanism. Although law itself operates at a conscious level, respect for it is partly due to this instinctive need for order. It is this instinctive need which, I suspect, explains the respect paid to law even in circumstances where respect for the law seems irrational. Such a proposition would require proof, which would be both difficult and lengthy and which would result in serious imbalance in this book; but I hope to return to the matter in a subsequent work.

(VI)

When I began this book I envisaged writing a final chapter on the nature of the obligation to obey the law. The course the book has taken makes such a chapter seem no longer necessary.

From the internal point of view, from the angle of those controlling the legal system, there is an obligation to obey the law simply because it is law. Seen from this standpoint the obligation to obey the law is a legal obligation. For philosophers, on the other hand, this would lead to an infinite regress:

> Since legal obligations derive from laws, there would have to be a law that says we must obey the law. What obligation would there then be to obey this law? If legal obligation, then there would have to be another law . . . and so on. If

> there is any obligation to obey the law it must, ultimately be a moral obligation.[22]

Where the law enjoins an act or abstention that is morally right, then the moral obligation so to act or abstain exists independently of the law. Where the law enjoins an act or abstention that is morally very wrong then the existence of the law cannot make the act or abstention morally right. (It is worth observing that a democratically elected government is no guarantee against thoroughly evil laws. For instance, a society that divides racially, or on religious grounds, into two groups may have a government elected in a properly democratic way that is dominated by the larger group and that by law then deliberately sets out to expropriate, force into exile or annihilate the minority.) Where the act or abstention enjoined by law is either morally neutral or marginally wrong, then the problem of a moral obligation to obey the law is reduced to two questions. First, what effect—and there need not be any—will disobedience have upon order? Secondly, if order will be affected by the disobedience, is order in this particular instance a good thing, or does it have such moral or social worth that its preservation outweighs the harm committed by the marginally immoral act?

This book has emphasised the process of law; it may be asked whether the question of duty in obeying the law might not be put more sharply in the form 'Is there a duty to obey a decision in the legal process?'[23] It is a characteristic of law that it is not always strictly enforced. In the situation now under discussion, the officers of the state have decided to take action. Someone who refuses to obey the court decision is thus setting himself in opposition to the state in a particularly strong way. The authority of the state is being strongly and directly challenged—not necessarily the case where one disobeys the law—and the effect on order is likely to be marked. Moreover, the disobedience of a court decision will be public in a way that is not usually true of disobedience of legal rule.

Notes and References

CHAPTER ONE

1. In the *Minos*, which is usually regarded as a close imitation of Plato's work by one of his disciples; see, e.g., A.-H. Chroust 'A note to the pseudo-Platonic dialogue *Minos*' *American Journal of Jurisprudence* 15 (1970) 171ff.
2. St Augustine's statements on Natural Law are scattered throughout his writings. For a summary of his view and citation of sources see H. A. Deans *The Political and Social Ideas of St. Augustine* (New York and London: Columbia University Press 1963), especially at pp.85-115.
3. See, e.g., *Summa Theologica*, quaest. 91,94.
4. Expressed clearly and succinctly in Cicero *de leg.* 1.6-12.
5. *Leviathan*, Part 1, chs. 14,15.
6. *De jure belli ac pacis* 1.1.10.
7. *Antigone* 450ff.
8. Exodus 1.17.
9. See also, in general, D. Daube *Civil Disobedience in Antiquity* (Edinburgh: University Press 1972).
10. *The Province of Jurisprudence Determined.*
11. Of which, apart from Hans Kelsen's *Pure Theory of Law*, the most famous is H. L. A. Hart *The Concept of Law* (Oxford: Clarendon Press 1961).
12. See also L. L. Fuller *The Morality of Law* 2nd ed. (New Haven and London: Yale University Press 1969) pp.191ff. The most compelling attack on the classic Positivist view is by Hart himself: *Concept of Law*. It should be said that at least the second of the above objections to the Positivists' view of law does not affect the Hartian variation.
13. See for this A. Watson *Society and Legal Change* (Edinburgh: Scottish Academic Press; Princeton: Princeton University Press, 1977). For appropriate references to Marx and his followers, see pp.3f; and see infra, pp.85f.
14. 889Eff.
15. 890C.
16. 338Cff; 343Aff.
17. *Politics*, 1296b35; 1320a4-1320b16; cf. 1281a37, 1282b10.
18. *Politics* 1296a16.

19. Indeed, Mr J. L. Barton points out to me that Austin was in fact secularising a view that was already ancient: 'The source of all law, properly speaking, is God. Since God has created man a social animal, it is in accordance with the will of God that man should organise himself into societies, and thus the powers that be are ordained of God. Thus we are bound to conscience, and not merely from prudence, to obey the command of a lawful superior, and *e contra*, the command of a lawful superior is necessary to make a good law which will bind our consciences. Austin takes the view that a society which does not possess a sovereign according to his definition has not yet emerged from the state of nature: a pointer to the sources which he was using. So Pufendorf, on whom Austin is relying to a great extent, relied in his turn upon the medieval theorists. He made the traditional doctrine palatable to an age which was no longer satisfied by its traditional justification by treating the question of sovereignty and subjection as depending upon fact rather than upon a higher law, but the doctrine that law must derive its binding force from the will of some legislator, and cannot be binding unless it be possible to identify some legislator who may be deemed to will it, whether expressly or by implication, has a very long history indeed.'
20. See, e.g., A. R. Radcliffe-Brown *Structure and Function in Primitive Society* (London: Cohen and West 1952) pp.12ff. R. K. Merton *On Theoretical Sociology* (New York: Free Press 1967) pp.74ff; *Social Theory and Social Structure*, enlarged ed. (New York: Free Press 1968) pp.74ff.
21. Radcliffe-Brown *Structure and Function*, p.180.
22. See, e.g., M. H. Lessnoff *The Structure of Social Science* (London: Allen and Unwin 1974) pp.109ff and the works he cites.
23. *Structure*, p.127. In a sense even classical functionalism is a variety of teleological argument, at least when it treats the consequences of patterns as (part of) their causes.
24. Yet, as J. Raz points out, legal theorists have paid surprisingly little attention to the elucidation of the notion of legal functions: 'On the functions of law' *Oxford Essays in Jurisprudence*, second series, ed. A. W. B. Simpson (Oxford: Clarendon Press 1973) pp.278ff at p.278.
25. *The Blue & Brown Books* 2nd ed. (Oxford: Blackwell 1969) p.87.
26. It should be noted that the essential function ascribed here to a car does not distinguish a car from other means of transporting people along roads. Nor will it be here claimed that the essential function of a human institution necessarily distinguishes it from other institutions.
27. I have produced this example to show what I mean by essential function, not because I think one can argue from the existence of an essential function for a car to the existence of an essential function of law. Some people who would accept the idea of an essential function of a man-made physical object might be reluctant to accept the idea of an essential function of a human institution.

28. My decision to use the adjective 'essential', which seems the most convenient for my purposes, coupled with the posing of the question 'What is law?' will suggest that I have adopted the methodology of the *realist* party—called the *essentialist* by Karl Popper—as distinct from that of the *nominalists*. Since I also believe that the social sciences must adopt a historical method in order to know a social group, such as a nation or race, I must concede that my approach is realist or essentialist, on Popper's terms. Popper takes a very poor view of essentialism; see, e.g., his *The Poverty of Historicism* 2nd ed. (London: Routledge & Kegan Paul 1961) and *The Open Society and its Enemies*, 2 vols. 5th ed. (London, Routledge & Kegan Paul 1965, 1966) *passim*. But since Popper declares that the problem at issue between the two parties, the *problem of universals*, is 'one of the oldest and most fundamental problems of philosophy' (*Poverty*, p.27) and that among social scientists there is no very energetic opposition to essentialism (*Poverty*, pp.29f), I hope it will be understandable and excusable if I do not feel obliged to justify methodological essentialism. But it does seem to me that the steps implicit in Popper's arguments against historicism are understandable only on what he considers an essentialist argument.
29. Thus, I will not list among the functions: 'To resolve the dispute with the specific object of social education'. This can certainly be a function of the legal process, and often is, perhaps especially in China. But no Western jurist would, I believe, consider it the essential function in the sense in which that term is used here.
30. For the strict functionalists, our number six would have to be rephrased as something like 'To resolve the dispute in such a way that further unregulated conflict is inhibited', or 'To resolve the dispute so that there is no disfunction through further unregulated conflict'. Some such reformulation would be necessary at various points in this chapter.
31. I am grateful to Mr Robert Black for this point. He also suggests that function two might better be expressed in a wider way: 'To resolve the dispute by applying the relevant rules of law, one of which *may* be that the facts should be established'.
32. See, above all, G. Neilson *Trial by Combat* (Glasgow: Hodge 1890).
33. *Brennu-Njáls Saga*, chapter 8. In the edition by E. O. Sveinsson (Reykjavik: Islenzk Fornrit 12, 1954) p.28; *Njal's Saga* translated by M. Magnusson and H. Pálsson (Harmondsworth: Penguin Books 1960) p.54.
34. Chapter 24; in Sveinsson's edition, p.67; in the translation by Magnusson and Pálsson, p.81.
35. Trial by battle has all the characteristics required for a legal process: see infra, pp.28f, 38f. Since, however, the substantive issues in dispute are not directly decided we might be tempted to see here a case of 'Law keeps out'; see infra, pp.96ff.

36. See for the rôle in tort actions of *inter alia* publicity, A. M. Linden 'Tort law as ombudsman' *Canadian Bar Review* 51 (1973) 155ff.
37. 'In order to'; the idea of purpose is necessary or in this type of situation the resulting violence would not be structured into the system, but would simply represent a particular failure of the essential function.

    For the immunity of trade unions in tort or delict—which may also be thought relevant here—see infra, pp.97ff.
38. See, e.g., K. N. Llewellyn 'Some realism about realism' in his *Jurisprudence, Realism in Theory and Practice* (Chicago: University Press 1962) pp.42ff at pp.53ff.
39. Llewellyn 'Realism', p.56.
40. See, e.g., W. E. Rumble *American Legal Realism* (Ithaca, N.Y.: Cornell University Press 1968) pp.137ff.
41. This 'section of the community' need not, of course, be a majority of the people.
42. See, e.g., M. Rheinstein *Marriage Stability, Divorce and the Law* (Chicago: University Press 1972) pp.56ff.
43. See, e.g., M. Kaser *Das römische Privatrecht* 1, 2nd ed. (Munich: Beck 1971) pp.728f.
44. See, e.g., W. W. Buckland *Textbook of Roman Law*, 3rd ed. by P. Stein (Cambridge: University Press 1963) p.512.
45. Chapter 123: translated by Magnusson and Pálsson, p.256; in the edition of Sveinsson, pp.314f.
46. *Society and Legal Change*, and see infra, pp.83ff.
47. We return to this topic, infra, pp.58ff.
48. See, for all, H. Maine *Ancient Law*, chapter 1.
49. For the channelling function of form in law, see L. L. Fuller 'Consideration and form' *Columbia Law Review* 41 (1941) 799ff at 801ff.

CHAPTER TWO

1. I use the term 'regulated sanction' to exclude mere social disapproval and unregulated violence.
2. *Roman Litigation* (Oxford: Clarendon Press 1966). For discussion of Kelly's views, see the reviews cited by G. MacCormack, 'Roman and African litigation' *T.v.R.* 39 (1971) 221ff at 223 nn. 7,8. And see for the Yurok Indians of California, A. L. Kroeber *Handbook of the Indians of California* (reprinted Berkeley: California Book Co. Ltd. 1953) p.22.
3. *The Law of Primitive Man* (Cambridge, Mass.: Harvard University Press 1954) pp.88f; see also pp.23ff for his discussion of what amounts to a court. His notion of a 'court' corresponds closely to what I mean by 'process', but he would place the situation described by Boas as just across the border-line into law.
4. *Law of Primitive Man*, p.25.
5. (London: Sweet & Maxwell 1924) p.39.
6. 12th ed. (London: Sweet & Maxwell 1966) pp.36f.
7. 'Groups, Laws, and Obedience' in *Oxford Essays in Jurisprudence*,

second series, ed. A. W. B. Simpson (Oxford: Clarendon Press 1973) pp.1ff at pp.3ff. Honoré elaborates his argument in 'What is a group?' *Archiv für Rechts- und Sozialphilosophie* 61 (1975) 161ff, but we need not here discuss his division of society into primary and secondary groups.

8. 'Groups, laws, and obedience', especially at p.19.
9. This suggestion relies upon the notion of a hierarchy of norm-creating authorities similar to that presented by Kelsen; but in using the conception of 'more powerful law' it applies a sociological test alien to Kelsen's pure theory.
10. For the purpose of this illustration the historical accuracy of this description of the Roman family council and the powers of the father is irrelevant, but see now A. Watson *Rome of the XII Tables, Persons and Property* (Princeton, N.J.: Princeton University Press 1975) pp.42ff.
11. See, e.g., J. Raz *The Concept of a Legal System* (Oxford: Clarendon Press 1970) p.1; contra, A. M. Honoré 'What is a group?'
12. Hans Kelsen *Pure Theory of Law* 2nd ed. trans. M. Knight (Berkeley and Los Angeles: University of California Press 1967).
13. *The Institutes of Law* 2nd ed. (Edinburgh and London: Blackwood 1880) pp.368f; see also, e.g., p.538.
14. *Of Laws in General*, ch. 2, i; see also supra, p.130, n.19.

CHAPTER THREE

1. *General Theory of Law and the State* trans. A. Wedberg (Cambridge, Mass: Harvard University Press 1946) p.111; cf. his *Pure Theory of Law* 2nd ed., trans. M. Knight (Berkeley, Los Angeles: University of California Press 1967) p.195.
2. *Concept of a Legal System* (Oxford: Clarendon Press 1970) p.1.
3. 'What is a group?' *Archiv für Rechts- und Sozialphilosophie* 61 (1975) 161ff at 161f.
4. 'The institutional nature of law' *MLR* 38 (1975) 489ff at 500ff.
5. The second is treated incidentally, infra pp. 52ff.
6. In fairness it must be remembered that for most jurists such rules would not be considered to be laws.
7. *The Province of Jurisprudence Determined* (first published in 1832) lecture VI; in the edition used (London: Weidenfeld and Nicolson 1954) p.193.
8. See, e.g., *Salmond on Jurisprudence* 12th ed. by P. J. Fitzgerald (London: Sweet & Maxwell 1966) pp.25ff; R. W. M. Dias *Jurisprudence*, 4th ed. (London: Butterworths 1976) pp.469ff; and the authors they cite.
9. See, e.g., M. Akehurst *Modern Introduction to International Law* 2nd ed. (London: Allen & Unwin 1971) pp.9ff.
10. e.g., *Province*, p.126.
11. *Concept of Law* (Oxford: Clarendon Press 1961) p.3.
12. See, e.g., Hart *Concept of Law*, pp.44ff.
13. See above all J. M. Kelly *Roman Litigation* (Oxford: Clarendon Press 1966) pp. 1ff.

14. See Hart *Concept of Law*, pp.33ff.
15. See, e.g., S. Lubman 'Mao and mediation: politics and dispute resolution in Communist China' *California Law Review* 55 (1967) 1284ff.
16. *Province*, p.195.
17. See, e.g., Akehurst *International Law*, pp.10f.
18. See, e.g., I. Zamir *The Declaratory Judgment* (London: Stevens 1962); S. A. de Smith *Constitutional and Administrative Law* 2nd ed. (Harmondsworth: Penguin 1973) pp.604ff; E. C. S. Wade and G. G. Phillips *Constitutional Law* 8th ed. by Wade and A. W. Bradley (London: Longman 1970) pp.671ff.

CHAPTER FOUR

1. See supra, pp. 45f.
2. Two instructive English cases turning on the Statutory Instruments Act, 1946, 2(1) and 3(2) are *Simmonds v. Newall* [1953] 1 W.L.R. 826 and *R. v. Sheer Metalcraft* [1954] 1 Q.B. 586.
3. *Fundamental Principles of the Sociology of Law* trans. W. L. Moll (Cambridge, Mass: Harvard University Press 1936) p.245.
4. *Laws* 4.722a.
5. For recent discussion for and against codification see, e.g., H. R. Hahlo 'Here Lies the Common Law: Rest in Peace' *MLR* 30 (1967) 241ff; A. L. Diamond 'Codification of the Law of Contract' *MLR* 31 (1968) 361ff; M. R. Topping and J. P. M. Vandenlinden '*Ibi renascit ius commune*' *MLR* 33 (1970) 170ff.
6. D. Daube 'The influence of interpretation on writing' *Buffalo Law Review* 20 (1970) 41ff at 46.
7. Daube, loc. cit.
8. J. Campbell *The Lives of the Chief Justices of England* 2 (London: Murray 1849) pp. 572f.
9. *The Morality of Law* 2nd ed. (New Haven and London: Yale University Press 1969) pp.33ff.

CHAPTER FIVE

1. *Memorabilia*, 1.2.40-46.
2. See for the U.S.A., L. L. Jaffe *English and American Judges as Lawmakers* (Oxford: Clarendon Press 1969) pp. 33f.
3. We need not here be more specific, but various forms of compromise including a division of territory can be envisaged.
4. And law itself is one weapon of the superior force.
5. For a discussion of validity, efficacy and existence of law see S. Munzer *Legal Validity* (The Hague: Nijhoff 1972) and the works he cites.
6. See, e.g., G. I. Tunkin *Theory of International Law* trans. W. E. Butler (London: Allen & Unwin 1974) pp.23ff, and the authors he cites.
7. Justice in International Law was understood not to be distributive.
8. See, on this, Tunkin *Theory*, pp.22ff.

9. See, in general G. G. Fitzmaurice 'The foundations of the authority of International law and the problem of enforcement' *MLR* 19 (1956) 1ff; I. Bibo *The Paralysis of International Institutions and the Remedies* (New York: Wiley 1976).
10. Although we need not go into it here there is dispute about the extent to which force in the wider sense of economic pressure should be excluded. The dispute indicates a tension in International law and relations between the ideal of equality of states and the fact of unequal power. See, e.g., J. J. Paust & A. P. Blaudstein 'The Arab oil weapon—a threat to international peace' *AJIL* 68 (1974) 410ff; I. F. I. Shihata 'Destination embargo of Arab oil: its legality under International law' *AJIL* 68 (1974) 591ff.
11. See, in general, Fitzmaurice 'Foundations'; I. M. Sinclair 'Principles of International law concerning friendly relations and co-operation among states' in *Essays on International Law in Honour of Krishna Rao* ed. M. K. Nawaz (Leyden: Sijthoff 1976) pp.107ff.
12. The theoretical framework of International law is very much a matter of dispute. I cannot pretend to expertise in the field and am greatly in the debt of Dr J. A. Carty whose generous help shaped the argument in this section.
13. See J. P. Casey 'The Genesis of the Dáil Courts' *Irish Jurist* 9 (1974) 326ff and the works he cites.

CHAPTER SIX

1. On law's function to channel and regulate behaviour see, e.g., K. N. Llewellyn 'The normative, the legal and the law-jobs: the problem of juristic method' *Yale Law Journal* 49 (1940) 1355ff.
2. This chapter derives from my book *Society and Legal Change* (Edinburgh: Scottish Academic Press; Princeton: Princeton University Press 1977), where the argument is set out in detail.
3. *De l'Esprit des Lois* (first published in 1748) book 1, ch. 3.
4. *System des heutigen römischen Rechts* 1 (Berlin: Veit 1840), p.14.
5. See, in general, O. Prausnitz *Standardization of Commercial Contracts in English and Continental Law* (London: Sweet & Maxwell 1937) p.20; for Scotland, Lord Cooper of Culross *Selected Papers, 1922-54* (Edinburgh: Oliver & Boyd 1957) p.199; for Spain, E. N. van Kleffens *Hispanic Law until the End of the Middle Ages* (Edinburgh: University Press 1968) p.28; for the Cherokee Indians, J. P. Reid *A Law of Blood, the Primitive Law of the Cherokee Nation* (New York: University Press 1970) p.3.
6. Actually longer, since one should date his attack on German codification to the first edition in 1814 of his *Vom Beruf unsrer Zeit für Gesetzgebung und Rechtswissenschaft.*
7. *Contemporary Juristic Theory* (Claremont, Calif.: Pomona College, Scripps College, Claremont College, 1940) pp.75f, 79ff.
8. See Marx-Engels *Die Deutsche Ideologie* book 3; *Manifesto of the Communist Party*, II; Marx's defence speech (1849) in Marx-Engels *Werke* 6 (Berlin: Dietz 1961) pp.244f.

9. Tumanov at the Georgian Conference on Law (1930); quoted by D. Lloyd *Introduction to Jurisprudence* 3rd ed. (London: Stevens 1970) p.670.
10. This goes back to Henry Maine whose *Ancient Law* was first published in 1861 (London: Murray); see also, e.g., A. S. Diamond *Primitive Law Past and Present* (London: Methuen 1971).
11. *Vom Beruf unsrer Zeit für Gesetzgebung und Rechtswissenschaft* 3rd ed. (Heidelberg: Mohr 1840) p.10.
12. Letter to C. Schmidt, dated October 27 1890, published in, e.g., Marx, Engels *Selected Works* (London: Lawrence & Wishart 1968) pp.684ff.
13. *Society and Legal Change.*
14. See D. Daube 'Three quotations from Homer in D.18.1.1.1' *CLJ* 10 (1949) 213ff.
15. On this and the remainder of this section see *Society and Legal Change*, pp.12ff.
16. [1961] A.C. 1090.
17. Report of the Committee on Defamation (London: H.M.S.O. 1975) Cmnd. 5909, 2.368, p.102.
18. The main sources are Tacitus *Annales*, 12.5ff; Gaius' *Institutes*, 1.62; *Codex Theodosianus*, 3.12.1. The second change in the law can scarcely be attributed to the influence of Christianity; see Watson *Society and Legal Change*, p.39.
19. The importance of the drafting of legislation being largely in the hands of lawyers is discussed infra, pp.99ff.
20. e.g., see *Society and Legal Change*, pp.87ff.

CHAPTER SEVEN

1. This statement is less true, but in general only to a very limited extent, of the law of a group other than territorial state. What is said in this chapter applies with minor modifications to such group laws.
2. *Vom Beruf unsrer Zeit für Gesetzgebung und Rechtswissenschaft* 3rd ed. (Heidelberg: Mohr 1840) pp.7f.
3. Even among lawyers very few are curious enough or informed enough to think of borrowing foreign rules. Knowledge of foreign systems is mostly professionally irrelevant, and hence not highly valued in modern law schools. The arguments of this chapter are set out in detail in my *Legal Transplants* (Edinburgh: Scottish Academic Press; Charlottesville, University Press of Virginia 1974).
4. Though it is found in Aristotle *Rhetorica* 1.13.3.
5. See, e.g., J. Austin *Jurisprudence* lecture 44 (in the 5th ed. by R. Campbell (London: Murray 1911) pp.744ff); G. Marty and P. Raynaud *Droit civil, 1, Introduction générale à l'étude du droit*, 2nd ed. (Paris: Sirey 1972) pp.65ff; H. P. de Vries *Civil Law and the Anglo-American Lawyer* (New York: Dobbs Ferry 1976) p.69; E. L. Johnson *Introduction to the Soviet Legal System* (London: Methuen 1969) pp.3ff.

6. See J. Schacht *Introduction to Islamic Law* (Oxford: Clarendon Press 1964) pp. 152, 154.
7. Cato, *de agri cultura* c.149.
8. e.g. Gaius' *Institutes* 3.141.
9. See, e.g., the *Practicks* of Sir James Balfour of Pittendreich 1 (Edinburgh: Stair Society 1962) pp.209ff.
10. 91 *LQR* (1975) 247ff.
11. At pp.254ff.
12. R. David 'The Civil Code in France today' *Louisiana Law Review* 34 (1974) 907ff; see also J. H. Merryman *The Civil Law Tradition* (Stanford: University Press 1969) pp.7,73. For the reception of Roman systematics into Scotland see my *Legal Transplants*, pp.36ff.
13. Admittedly much modern law reform by transplanting is done in a more scholarly fashion.
14. *ad familiares* 7.10.
15. See A. Kocourek 'Factors in the reception of law' *Studi in memoria di A. Albertoni* 3 (Padua: Cedam 1938) 233ff.
16. The *Digest*, though, is no model of arrangement. In view of the existence of the *Institutes* this was a matter of less concern.
17. Some parts were in Greek. These were not read or lectured on, hence the law in them was not influential.
18. There was for a time an exception in Louisiana and partial exceptions in, for instance, Texas.
19. See, above all, J. S. Waterman 'Thomas Jefferson and Blackstone's *Commentaries*' now in *Essays in the History of Early American Law* ed. D. H. Flaherty (Chapel Hill: University of North Carolina Press 1969) pp.451ff.
20. Waterman 'Jefferson', p.452.
21. See, e.g., J. Limpens 'Territorial expansion of the Code' in *The Code Napoleon and the Common Law World* ed. B. Schwartz (New York: University Press 1956) pp.92ff.
22. B. Pooley 'The modernization of law in Ghana' in *Ghana and the Ivory Coast* ed. P. Foster and A. R. Zolberg (Chicago and London: Chicago University Press 1971) pp.167ff at p.172.
23. This, of course, does not mean that two-thirds of Scots law was borrowed straight from England. Other factors can also account for some of the legal similarities.
24. See, for more detail, Watson *Legal Transplants*, pp.44ff: 'The rise of modern Scots Law' *La Formazione storica del diritto moderno in Europa* 3 (Florence: Olschki 1977) 1167ff.
25. Louisianans mostly regard these doubts as belonging to the past, largely thanks to the efforts of the Louisiana State Law Institute. See, e.g., M. E. Barham 'Renaissance of civilian tradition in Louisiana' in *The Role of Judicial Decisions and Doctrine in Civil Law and In Mixed Jurisdictions* ed. J. Dainow (Baton Rouge: Louisiana State University Press 1974) pp.38ff.
26. See, e.g., A. Tate 'The role of the judge in mixed jurisdictions: the Louisiana experience' in *Judicial Decisions and Doctrine*, pp.23ff.

27. The Louisiana State Law Institute has been active in translating civil law material.
28. According to H. R. Hahlo: 'If the civil law of Quebec has shown itself more resistant to the pervasive influences of the common law than the Roman-Dutch law of South Africa, this has been largely due to the fact that it was contained in a code, whereas the Roman-Dutch law was not' from 'Here lies the common law: rest in peace' *MLR* 30 (1967) pp.241ff at pp.243f. The experience of Louisiana suggests that Hahlo exaggerates the importance of codification in this regard.
29. *Europa und das römische Recht* (Munich: Biederstein 1947) pp.137f.
30. See A. Watson 'Legal transplants and law reform' *LQR* (1976) pp.79ff; *Society and Legal Change* (Edinburgh: Scottish Academic Press; Princeton: Princeton University Press 1977) pp.98ff. For a different view see, e.g., O. Kahn-Freund 'On uses and misuses of comparative law' *MLR* 37 (1974) pp.1ff.
31. See, e.g. J. H. Beckstrom 'Transplantation of legal systems: an early report on the reception of Western laws in Ethiopia' *American Journal of Comparative Law* 21 (1973) 557ff; J. Starr and J. Pool 'The impact of a legal revolution in rural Turkey' *Law and Society Review* 8 (1974) 534ff.
32. I do not mean, of course, that a society should not strive for the most suitable rules.

CHAPTER EIGHT

1. See, e.g., R. Hogan and C. Mills 'Legal socialization' *Human Development* 19 (1976) 261ff.
2. From the prologue to the law code, trans. S. N. Kramer in J. B. Pritchard *Ancient Near Eastern Texts Relating to the Old Testament* 3rd ed. (Princeton: University Press 1969) p.159.
3. Translated by T. J. Meek in Pritchard *Ancient Near Eastern Texts*, p. 178.
4. 9.95ff, trans. A. T. Murray, 1 (London, Cambridge, Mass.: Loeb Classical Library 1946) p.389.
5. 1.94, trans. C. H. Oldfather, 1 (London, Cambridge, Mass.: Loeb Classical Library 1960) p.321. See also Herodotus *Hist.* 1.65; Plutarch *Lycurgus* 5.3; Plato *Laws* 1 (p.624); Plutarch *De se citra invidiam laudando* 11.
6. 2.61, trans. E. Cary, 1 (London, Cambridge, Mass.: Loeb Classical Library 1966) p.489.
7. Exodus 20.
8. Exodus 18.13ff.
9. The oldest known Code is that of Ur-Nammu who founded the third dynasty of Ur. Not enough is known of this king to account him a great leader.
10. See C. G. Gadd in *The Cambridge Ancient History* 2, 3rd ed. (Cambridge: University Press 1973) pp.176ff.
11. Suetonius *Divus Julius*, 44.2; Isidorus *Etymologiae*, 5.1.5.

12. Quoted by B. Schwartz in *The Code Napoleon and the Common-Law World* (New York: University Press 1956) p.vii. I regret that I have been unable to trace the ultimate source of the quotation.
13. The translation is that of F. W. Kelsey (Oxford: Clarendon Press 1925).
14. D.1.1.1pr, 1; 1.1.10.2.
15. See A. Watson *Society and Legal Change* (Edinburgh: Scottish Academic Press; Princeton: Princeton University Press 1977) at, e.g., pp.12ff, 31ff, 47ff.
16. Pseudo-Platonic dialogue *Minos*.
17. A. H. Campbell has rightly observed that, even within a state, ideas of morality may vary from one locality to another: 'Obligation and obedience to law' *Proceedings of the British Academy* 51 (London: Oxford University Press 1965) 337ff at 338f.
18. See, e.g., L. L. Fuller *Morality of Law* 2nd ed. (New Haven and London: Yale University Press 1969).
19. See now, e.g., A. Watson *Rome of the XII Tables* (Princeton: University Press 1975) p.74.
20. On the question of differentiation in life and differentiation in law see D. Daube *Roman Law: Linguistic, Social, and Philosophical Aspects* (Edinburgh: University Press 1969) pp.157ff.
21. See, e.g., S. Plawski *Étude des principes fondamentaux du droit international pénal* (Paris: Pichon & Durand-Auzias 1972) p.7.
22. P. Singer *Democracy and Disobedience* (Oxford: Clarendon Press 1973) p.3.
23. See already D. Daube *Civil Disobedience in Antiquity* (Edinburgh: University Press 1972) p.77.

Index